A Place of Springs

PSALM 84:5,6

"Blessed are the men whose strength is in thee;

... as they go through the valley of Baca they

make it a place of springs."

A Place of Springs

VIOLA GOODE LIDDELL

THE UNIVERSITY OF ALABAMA PRESS
UNIVERSITY, ALABAMA

ACKNOWLEDGMENTS

I would like to express my gratitude to the many friends and relatives who allowed me to use incidents about themselves or their families in order to paint a word picture of a peculiar people as they are driven by forces beyond their control and not of their choosing from a beleaguered position of self-reliant, and often defiant, isolation following the Civil War into the national and global maelstrom of twentieth-century life.

My gratitude extends also to my immediate family who graciously allowed me time from my domestic duties to do the work and to the faithful black hands that assumed many of those duties, thereby making the task a joyous and rewarding one.

Finally, I must thank Macmillan Inc. for permission to quote from William Butler Yeats's poem "The Second Coming," *Collected Poems,* copyright © 1924 by Macmillan Publishing Company, copyright renewed 1952.

Viola Goode Liddell

Second printing, first paperback edition, 1982

Library of Congress Cataloging in Publication Data

Liddell, Viola Goode, 1901–
    A place of springs.

    1. Camden, Ala.—Social life and customs. 2. Lid-
dell, Viola Goode, 1901–   3. Camden, Ala.—Biography.
4. Afro-Americans—Alabama—Camden. I. Title.
F334.C25L53   976.1'38   78-31572
ISBN 0-8173-0121-6

Contents

Foreword

One cannot love a thing unless it calls for loving, nor sympathize with it unless there is some need. One does not understand a place or its people until the living sights and sounds of them be sifted through the heart.

Thus I write of a passing scene, of a people needing love and understanding even while denying the need of anything, of a people whom I love not only for their great goodness and for their sometimes grievous faults but because they are my people and I am one of them.

The heroine of my story is a small Black Belt town whose visible features are Southern rural, but whose core and conscience are singularly Black Belt: proud, provincial, conservative, whimsical, with the bearing of a great lady until displeased, then displaying the temper of a shrew; farsighted for things of the past but purblind to the tides of change washing about her; stouthearted as Job from carrying burdens too heavy for her, but near addlepated from trying to remain the stationary center of the universe; clinging desperately to the crumbling walls of chivalry and the Puritan Ethic with one hand and with the other defiantly defending her right to go to hell if she pleases; bighearted as all outdoors to those whom she claims as her own, but for those whom she considers meddling outsiders, may the Lord have mercy on their souls.

A Place of Springs

ONE

A Journey Begun

Occasional swirls of devil-dust danced down the red-graveled road and careened across the ashen hedgerows to settle on the scorched fields beyond. Corn, matured early, stood in parchment-colored patches like congregations of stringy-haired crones, whispering together. Pungent whiffs of a clothy odor hung in the air near the cotton fields, which stood drooping and yellowing from thirst.

Here a wagon, loaded with cotton, groaned wearily on its way to the gin, wobbly wheels making serpentine tracks in the dust; there another bounced and clattered emptily by, hurrying home to shade and water. Now and again an impatient car honked loudly from behind and, swooshing by as I pulled over, left miles of trailing dust hanging over the road ahead. When at length the dust drifted away, a shimmering haze of heat, making water-puddle mirages over the road, rose to meet the snowy islands of clouds hanging in the sky.

For days the clouds had come and gone, tantalizing, irritatingly near, and not delivering on a single promise of rain. But it was September. Dry and hot. And until the cotton was safely ginned, the farmers preferred it that way. Clean dry cotton upgraded to middling; dirty damp cotton downgraded to low-middling or low. No matter how mightily people of the Black Belt might suffer and complain about the heat and dust of late summer, nobody with the sense of a dusting doodle wanted it to rain from August to November. For, as cotton went, so went his livelihood. Thus it had been since time immemorial.

But in the fall of this particular year of 1933 there was little concern for whether it rained or not, for the scrappy crops were hardly worth harvesting. It seemed as if Nature herself, weary of producing more and more only to have it worth less and less, had at last decided that a bountiful crop was no longer worthwhile. Cotton five cents a pound, cows ten, corn fifty cents a bushel. After years of pernicious anemia, the ultimate debilitation was finally descending like the plague on the whole area. Emaciated, beggared, paralyzed—once again a long-burdened people staggered helplessly and, what was worse, hopelessly, on the edge of a cataclysm reminiscent of Reconstruction days.

For years on end the Good Lord had seen fit to watch, apparently unmoved, his benighted likenesses in the Southland turning on the spit; but now at last since His long-pampered Up-Easterners were jumping out of windows and blowing their brains out because of the stock-market crash, and because his cross-country Westerners were hollering to high heaven about their land values' collapsing and their banks all closing, Southerners were beginning to hope that He would take notice and pass a miracle on the whole lot of us, seeing as how it had at last been pretty well proven that one part of a people could hardly keep on getting richer and richer while the other part was slowly starving to death.

True, instead of looking to heaven, some folks looked to Washington, where the great magician Franklin Delano Roosevelt had promised everybody, starting with the little man who had the least, a New Deal. But days had passed into weeks and weeks into months and this magical mover of men's minds and hearts had failed to get his legerdemain to working. With Congress his slow and clumsy assistant, coins pulled out of an empty hat in Washington had not trickled down to Podunk, U.S.A. To thousands with idle hands and empty bellies one thing seemed sure; unless some deal—old, new, or otherwise—began working some magic soon, there would be precious few left to work it on.

Although I had not yet joined the hungry, I could not help but wonder and worry as I bumped along the rutty road, wonder what I would do without money until my promised school teacher's pay of eighty-five dollars a month would come due a month hence, worry for fear my salary would be paid in warrants, as it had been the previous year, and that school would not last until Christmas. Fortunately, the past year my landlady had accepted teachers' warrants for room and board, as the groceryman accepted them from her for food. But no one else, not even the banks, would cash them. Sure, they were as sound as the great state of Alabama, but the great state of Alabama wasn't worth the paper its great seal was stamped on. Not now. Had the Indians returned to Alabama in 1933 they might have bought back the whole state for a string of wampum. And where, people asked, had all the money gone that had floated around so freely in the late twenties? For sure, no one I knew well enough to ask for a loan had any.

But with a Macawberlike faith I could still believe that this beg-and-barter sort of existence would not last forever and that somehow for me the future would be better than the past. Hoping that I had acquired a modicum of hard sense going up fool's hill, I resolved that, come what might, I would commit my efforts to hastening any possible improvement in my far from enviable condition.

TWO
_____

The River Road—Long Past

Suddenly the road topped a winding hill and below, near the abandoned crossing known as Miller's Ferry, arched the graceful Lee Long Bridge, spanning a serpentine, green-fringed ribbon of glass—the Alabama River. Draining the red hills of North Georgia, source waters of this stream converge into the Coosa and Tallapoosa Rivers of North East Alabama; these unite in the central part of the state to form the Alabama, which in turn joins the Tombigbee-Warrior system of West Alabama, all at last gathering their waters into the Mobile River and thence flowing into Mobile Bay and the Gulf of Mexico.

Once a highway for Indian pirogues and canoes, later for pioneer rafts and keelboats, the Alabama became in the early 1800s a red carpet for the River Queens that churned languidly and hooted dolefully through Alabama's cotton kingdom, taking out the white gold and bringing in whatever the kingdom needed to sustain and enhance it, from plows and pins to Italian marble and Parisian gowns.

Though the iron and steam monsters that later came thundering through the land gradually replaced the River Queens, they could not erase the marks or memories of these gentler, water-bound travelers. But as the years of the 1900s marched along, the river's usefulness so declined that the stream was considered more of a nuisance than a boon, a formidable barrier slicing the county of Wilcox into two parts and a devilishly crooked line for school children to reproduce on their geography maps.

When at last a steel and concrete bridge had spanned the barrier and linked the county's parts, the river was largely ignored—that is, so long as it slept peacefully. And sleep it did most of the time, unmindful of change or time or season, or of man's indifference to itself.

But occasionally, when rains fell for days without ceasing, the engorged river would push out of its banks, sometimes swiftly, sometimes slowly, but always relentlessly, spreading death and destruction like a creeping plague over everything that lived or grew in the rich lowlands along its course. Even at such times, viewing its deceptively demure surface, dancing and shimmering in the sunlight, one could hardly conceive of the vicious, ruthless, deep-down current, which, quietly and unseen, like a powerful catharsis, swept before it everything less powerful than itself. At such times people cursed the river as a dispensation of the devil, never dreaming that out of such power might come good as well as ill.

Camden, the county seat of Wilcox County since 1832, was the small town to which fate had decreed I go. Both town and county had been and would continue to be inexorably fashioned by their linkage to this ample and everlasting stream. Because of the river's tortuous course through its diagonal dimension, Wilcox could boast of, or deplore, as the case might be, more miles of river frontage than any other county in the state and more river landings during the steamboat days. These eighty-four old landings bear the names of pioneer families, of ferries, bluffs and bends which, once bywords, will for years to come sprinkle the conversation of native inhabitants: Yellow Jacket, Prairie, Walnut and Hurricane Bluffs; Tait's, Burford's, Ellis, and Bridgeport Landings; Cobb's and Miller's Ferries, and many more. Once bustling points of traffic and travel, now largely obliterated by the onslaught of time and change, they are still bleak reminders of a past, brightly embroidered by nostalgia, that will long be cherished as a sort of gone-with-the-wind glory.

Built for speed, beauty, and business, these River Queens, often called and quite often miscalled Floating Palaces, were handmaidens of King Cotton and, with the affluence of the antebellum era, were pacesetters for the social and economic life of the Black Belt of Alabama in those halcyon days. Some, with swept-back smoke stacks, decked out in fancy gingerbread trim, were two hundred and more feet long and boasted six boilers. The pilot house perched atop the Texas, which housed the officers; below the Texas were the passenger deck and quarters; near water level, the freight deck with its cargo and crew of Negro deck hands.

The early riverboats were usually side-wheelers with powerful machinery, often pushed to dangerous and explosive pressures by heart pine fed into their fireboxes—plus fatback or pure resin when a race or delayed schedule demanded maximum speed. The later boats were oftener stern-wheelers, which were considerably more dangerous in the unpredictable river waters. A special and exclusive whistle, a sort of trademark for each boat, elicited great pride and might foster envy among captains and pilots, while a calliope—if the boat was so prosperous as to boast one—furnished gay tunes for dockings or any other festive occasion.

Business trips, vacations, honeymoons, house parties, gambling sessions—whatever the occasion for taking the boat—the leisurely pace allowed ample time for making acquaintances, promoting romances, and cementing lifelong friendships. There were many memorable boats plying the Alabama River, but the most enviable was the *Nettie Quill,* with its intrepid and affable owner, Captain John Quill. She was painted white with golden crowns on her smokestacks and her twenty-one staterooms opened onto a spacious, carpeted saloon cabin. Her bar served the best liquors and her food was renowned. Even the quarters for the deckhands were comfortable and pleasant.

Hunters and fishermen up and down the river furnished Captain Quill with much of the fish and game for his packet in exchange for ammunition and sto'-bought delicacies. One of these hunters was an old Negro named Si Samson. Si always waited for the *Nettie Quill* around the mouth of Bear Creek with whatever he had for the captain's larder, and if the boat came in at night he would flag her down with a lighted lantern.

One cold winter night when the *Nettie Quill* was fighting her way upstream against a driving, freezing rain, Captain Quill saw Si's lantern light frantically waving around in a circle. Difficult as it was to put in to shore, Captain Quill made for the bank and went out into the sleety rain to get what he expected to be a gunny sack of quail or squirrel. When near enough to be heard, Captain Quill yelled to Si. "What in hell's creation have you got on a devilish night like this?"

"I got you a 'coon, Boss," answered Si hopefully.

"A 'coon? You damn-fool nigger," swore the Captain, "don't you know a 'coon ain't fit to eat?"

"They're fine," Si assured him. "You jes try this 'un and see."

"Hell, no," Captain Quill bawled back at him. "Why I'd sooner eat a dog."

"I'm sorry," said Si mournfully, "but I guess it all depends on how a pusson was fotch up. Now, myself, I'd ruther eat a 'coon."

There was intense rivalry among many of the boats, among crews, pilots, and even their passengers. Captains indulged in cutrate fares and freight rates; competition led to bitterness, brawls, and violence. One such incident occurred between Bob Otis of the *St. Charles* and James Green of the *F. P. Kimball.* The two captains, having slashed fares to a meager two dollars and a half for a trip of four hundred miles and two days' duration from Mobile to Montgomery, left Mobile in high dudgeon. Near Claiborne, the *St. Charles,* in the act of passing the *Kimball,* bore down upon it, causing it to swing heavily to shore. Captain Otis, later claiming protection of his boat and crew, drew his gun and fired point-blank at the pilot of the *Kimball,* who was badly, though not mortally, wounded.

The rivalry among the queens for transporting cargo and passengers, however, could not compare with their rivalry in the matter of speed. The number of boilers, the draught of the vessel, the stroke of the engines, its load and number of stops, as well as other variants, determined the time needed to complete a trip. But slicing off a few hours from a schedule was a source of great boasting—a feat calling for minute comparisons and a variety of explanations both factual and fanciful.

Most of the boat races that were held for no other reason than to determine which was the boat of greater speed, took place nonstop between the mouth of the Mobile River and the confluence of the Alabama and the Tombigbee, fifty miles upstream. Mobs crowded the wharf at Mobile as the passenger-crammed vessels set out. Smaller boats followed to learn the outcome and return the second day. On the third day an account of the race was headlined in the *Mobile Register.* Among the jubilant crew and passengers, the proud owners and prouder builders, of the victorious vessel were many who returned richer by thousands of dollars or perhaps a plantation or a race horse or two.

But river travel had its many hazards: sandbars, snags, shifting channels, high water that hid landmarks and shallow water that barely covered treacherous shoals. Catastrophes were frequent. Wilcox County waters entomb the remains of many of these old vessels and their human cargo. There was the *Senator No. 2,* which blew up and sank at Young's Landing; the *C. W. Dorrance,* running in a fog, which hit the wreckage and sank on top of it. The *Joab Lawrence* sank at Yellow Jacket Bluff, the *Commodore Farrand* at Packer's Bend, the *Jewess* at Prairie, and the *Orleans St. John* off Hurricane Bluff. An unidentified craft lying upstream from Hurricane Bluff is thought to have been a slave ship, which, if ever salvaged, might be found to have skeletons of slaves shackled in its hold.

The *Orleans St. John,* sunk in March 1850, was thought to carry dust and ingots of California gold. Though salvage operations on this boat by William Harris failed to discover the gold, hundreds of other items were found in a remarkable state of preservation: china glazed with the boat's name, stacks of melted coins, chunks of melted brass, shoes, children's dresses, corsets, books (scorched but still legible), hay (still retaining its original color), and even lumps of mule dung. Of the sixty passengers aboard, only twenty survived. One who might otherwise have survived was crushed by a trunk thrown overboard as he attempted to rescue a mother and child.

But collisions and explosions and loss of life did not stop these doughty captains. River life for them was not only exciting but profitable. And it was King Cotton that kept them and their boats afloat. The *James T. Staples* once moved five thousand bales of cotton on its decks and on barges, lashed alongside and in tow, from Selma to Mobile. Many boats cleared as much as $75,000 in one season, most of it cotton freight.

Owners of river landings provided warehouses with stalls, rented by merchants and landowners, where merchandise, brought up by boat, might be stored until wagons could haul it out to inland stores and commissaries. A windlass, usually fashioned from a massive tree-trunk mounted upright to turn on a stationary core, and operated like a syrup mill by a mule hitched to a beam inserted cross-wise, wound up the cable, which in turn hauled up a triangular carriage loaded with luggage and freight.

The bales of cotton were rolled down a ramp or cleared place on the riverbank and caught below by sweating, swearing or singing roustabouts. The passengers walked to and from the boat by way of a flight of steps extending from water's edge to level ground above. Possibly a record for such a flight—three hundred and sixty-five steps—was held by Claiborne Landing in Monroe County.

The proprietors of these river gateways had of necessity to provide food and lodging for outgoing passengers awaiting a boat or for those incoming who could not reach their destinations because of boggy roads or inclement weather. The impatience of these delayed passengers often drove these good people to near distraction. One such at old Bridgeport Landing, Mister Wirt Moore—who would never allow a male either doddering old or shirt-tail young to sit at his dining table without a coat—was once bedeviled by a nervous young man on his way to his wedding as to when the overdue boat would arrive. Not being a diviner of anything so chancy as a steamboat's timetable, Mister Moore advised patience and calm. And as the day progressed, more of the same. After six distressful hours a boat sounded up the river. The prospective bridegroom, at last hopeful, rushed to inquire of Mister Moore how long it would take the boat to arrive after its whistle was heard from around the bend.

Mister Moore eyed him in exasperation. "Son," he said, "I wouldn't rightly know. One blew around that bend twenty-five years ago, and it ain't got here yet."

THREE
_____

The River—Recent Past

Even after the iron-horses came snorting through the land, and after men learned to throw the abundant gravel lying alongside the roads into quagmires of mud and render them passable, the river still had to be crossed; and the few bridges that spanned the Alabama were necessary links of strategic highways usually on the doorsteps of our cities. So, until 1931, when the Lee Long Bridge was completed, there were only two ways to cross the river in Wilcox County, by skiff when the water was out of its banks or by ferry when it was within them.

Well do I recall how negotiating the steep treacherous banks and manipulating the deliberate, cable-guided, current-propelled boat required half an hour if the current was strong and the "flat" was on the right side of the river, the right side being the side on which the traveler arrived. But if the flat happened to be on the opposite side, or if the ferryman had to be hallooed out of his sleep, or if the current was sluggish and poling necessary, crossing could rarely be accomplished in under an hour.

Vivid in my memory is a picture of my father preparing on a cold winter day for this twenty-mile trip from our home to the county seat, the same trip I was now taking in so different a manner: a team of horses hitched to his buggy, storm curtains up, father cocooned in overcoat, earmuffs, and gloves lined with rabbit fur. Over his knees was a heavy laprobe. Mother would put heated bricks wrapped in flannel into the foot of the buggy for keeping his feet warm, and father made sure he carried in his pocket a nip of Four Roses with which to fortify himself later in the day.

These trips—to serve on the jury, to consult a lawyer, to pay his taxes, to attend a funeral, or to get the political lay of the land—were in wintertime, with prairie mud often hub-deep, sunup to sundown excursions with the river always a formidable barrier midway. If lucky, father would arrive in Camden by midafternoon, take his team to the livery stable and settle down either with a friend or at the wood-framed Boltz Hotel or the paint-peeled brick Wilcox Hotel, where, until it was replaced by a motel, summer patrons were told to leave their windows and doors open at night so that they might get a breeze from the big fans mounted in the cross-corridors.

But if, when he set out, the river was out of its banks, arrangements had to be made for him to be met from the other side, his buggy and team returned by a driver, and he taken across the river in a skiff with a good paddleman who could outmaneuver the treacherous current. And woe to anyone caught across river by flood water. The team would be stranded, and the trip back would be a two-day affair of seventy cindery, snail-slow miles by rail, broken by a night's layover in Selma, a quiet, serene little city in the neighboring county of Dallas.

One of the greatest dangers of crossing the river in those days was that the horses and mules in transit might become frightened and back off the flat or charge forward into the restraining timbers thrown across the forward end of the flat, either to injure themselves or damage the vehicle. And the danger of losing one's conveyance not only did not lessen, but actually increased, with the advent of the gasoline buggy.

These balky and contrary contraptions were for many years the bane of the ferryman's existence. They frightened the animals taken onto the flat in their company, so that rearing, plunging animals were commonplace. The drivers, no more adjusted to manipulating these new machines than the animals were to confronting them, were forever hitting the flat too hard coming on, and kicking it out from under the hind wheels, which inevitably burrowed into wet earth, subsequently having to be bodily pried or lifted out.

Or the brakes would fail or the driver forget to put them on—or put his foot on the accelerator instead—the machine dashing across the flat and crashing into the protecting timbers. Occasionally the barrier would fail to hold, and the car plow through it and plunge into the river. The driver was usually able to scramble out, not a difficult feat in the days of open cars, and later, with winches, cables, and mules, to salvage his waterlogged machine.

One such incident proved a sad climax to an otherwise happy occasion, when an inexperienced driver with his first car and a new and overly trusting wife, who chose to ride rather than walk onto the flat, crashed the barrier and plunged into the river. As the bridegroom extricated himself from the car and climbed onto the flat, he saw his bride floundering in the nearby water, apparently on the verge of drowning. Either frightened or unable to swim, it is not known which, the young man made no effort to rescue his wife, but instead snatched a dollar bill from his pocket and, waving it in the air, screamed to the ferryman and other passengers present, "Save my wife! A dollar for my wife! A dollar for my wife!"

Extending his pushing pole out to the victim, the ferryman so easily rescued the dripping, sputtering bride that even the one dollar reward was withheld until laughing passengers demanded it be paid. Then, as one passenger later related it, the irate bride, vowing she'd not be caught dead with a man who valued her life so lightly, took off her shoes and, in spite of apologies and remonstrations from her mate, stoically set out for home as determinedly as bare feet could take her.

To the danger of getting on and off the flat was often added the danger of getting up and down the steep and often muddy banks. Because of this danger, and also to help lighten the car's load, most passengers left their vehicles at the first declivity and did not reenter them until their drivers had brought them safely to the top of the opposite bank.

Because of such precautions, more than one man became involved in a dilemma that might mean spending days in the doghouse. One such occurred in my own family. Mr. Berry, a brother-in-law, and his none-too-slender wife Mary (whom we called Mamie) were crossing over one hot summer's day. Doubting both her husband's driving and the car's ability to get up the river bank with her inside, Mamie walked down the near bank and, after the flat was moored, began to plod and puff up the opposite bank. Mr. Berry did what was customary, gave his little flivver the juice, bounded off the flat, and striving to stay in the ruts by never slackening his pace, sped up to level ground without mishap. But so concerned had he been with maneuvering the vehicle and accomplishing his goal unhindered, that he joyously raced fifteen miles on down the road to Camden, completely unaware of his spouse's predicament.

Arriving home, he was met by his son, whose first words were "Papa, where's Mama?"

"Where's Mama?" Mr. Berry repeated vacantly.

It was a good question, and one that was repeated often through the years, always to Mr. Berry's chagrin and dismay.

The placid canoe-days long a legend, the grand steamboat-days a faded memory, the hazardous ferry-days now happily past, cars now slid over a slim rainbow of concrete and steel as smoothly as water drops down a window pane. For travelers, the Alabama River was at last impotent, no longer a divider of things for people of Wilcox County. For the city dwellers up above, it had become a sort of sluggish intestine to eliminate their wastes; to the fisherman and bargeman it was a lonely trail in which to ply their trade; but to those in the Black Belt who loved her and went to her for solace and renewal of spirit, the queen of the cotton kingdom had become a sort of Sleeping Beauty. However, there were a few daydreamers, visionaries, even in the year 1933, who knew that the Alabama was not really a sleeping beauty but rather a Sleeping Giant— one that would someday be wakened and whose powerful sinews would then be harnessed to shake and to remake this quiet, drowsy land.

But for me, this dry September day, crossing over the river so easily, so quickly, seemed an omen, and a good one. Things *did* change, and for the better. Perhaps after wandering around in an unreal world in which I had never felt a real part, this time, this place, was to be a divider in my life, a divider between the unreal and the real. With the severance of my roots I had, as it were, found no sustenance in far-off places; with one transplanting after another and ever set in shallower and more barren soil, I had borne neither foliage nor fruit.

Maybe at last back in my swaddling world where every odor, sight, and sound rang bells that made the sort of melody I understood—even if at times doleful and out of tune—whose people were my people, whose plight was my plight, maybe life would become real at last, and I might put down roots that would live and grow.

Yet with all my hope, even to clutching at signs and omens, I was dubious. I was almost afraid. Although the river had separated me from it as a child, I had lived too close to this little county-seat town of Camden and had heard too much about it—and much of what I had heard had not endeared it to me.

Even so, there were friends and kin there. There was good there, too. Perhaps I would be lucky enough to find my share. What I did not realize at the time was that news of the ugly and foolish things a man does travels fast and far, while the good he does creeps about slowly and unheralded, if indeed it ever travels beyond his own fireside.

FOUR

Destination

Without actually being on the river, Camden was, and still is, a sort of river town. First named Barboursville, it was often called Shaverstown and its youngsters "little shavers," until the unhappy town fathers decided to change the name to Camden in deference to a Dr. John Caldwell whose native home was Camden, South Carolina.

It sits near the center of a narrow neck of land where the Alabama River, after circling in a forty-mile loop, almost bites off the big bend held in its embrace. In steamboat days a traveler could leave his boat in the morning at one neck-side landing, come into town, attend to business or visit friends, then go to the opposite neck-side landing in the afternoon, catch the same boat and continue on his journey.

Traveling across this bend, known as Canton Bend, I had time to recall some of the stories I had heard in former years about Camden, the county seat of my native county—stories which, though told at random and out of context perhaps, had nevertheless colored the picture I had formed of this little town.

There were stories of the days when the town was "wide open," when a liquor dispensary did a thriving business, the whiskey being hauled from the river in barrels over the road that to this day is known as Whiskey Run Road. During these early pre-Prohibition days, when it was not unusual or disgraceful for a man to shoot another man in defense of his pride or his honor, it was considered dangerous for a woman to be out on the streets after dark, and on Saturday nights houses were locked, shades were drawn, and women and children huddled near their own firesides awaiting the midnight arrival of their menfolk, who did not close their businesses until the last possible customer had disappeared from the streets.

Although considerable real brawling and violence regularly occurred on Saturday nights—not the least of which was razor-slashings and knife-stabbings among the Negroes—engendering fear in the law-abiding populace, there was something else that struck terror into the hearts of those living on the main streets of the community. The more obstreperous young swains (whose evening attire commonly included pistols, which were removed from their persons only in deference to the wishes of their female companions, as men now check their hats and overcoats) got their "kicks" by racing their horses pell-mell up and down the streets, yip-yipping at the top of their lungs and shooting their forty-fours into the air at intervals along the way. These nocturnal forays not only sounded like sudden Comanche raids, but one never knew whether they were "for real" or not, or when too much liquor might cause a bullet to go astray, with terrifying results.

It is still told with some pride how one of these young men proved his expert marksmanship by shooting, from horseback, the doorknob off the schoolhouse door, some fifty yards away, though of necessity this was accomplished in daylight. Also that another, in playful mood, rode his horse into the drugstore and demanded that the proprietor feed his mount an ice-cream cone, and that the proprietor himself eat a sardine from the barrel of his pistol. Needless to say, both demands were complied with, much to the delight of everyone present except the proprietor himself.

There was another story about a daylight encounter of one of these daredevils with a stranger in town who had no way of knowing that this pistol-waving dervish was not taking pot-shots at him. Scared within an inch of his life at such an escapade, the stranger, toting a pistol himself and being adept in its use, responded to what he assumed was an attack on his life by shooting the pommel off the prankster's saddle, thereby giving him the shock of his young life. That particular episode, it was said, considerably "damped down" this kind of hell-raising. Later these same young men would raise a more sophisticated kind of hell, again shocking their elders out of their wits, by splitting the wind in Stutz Bear Cats and Stanley Steamers at the prodigious speed of thirty miles an hour. Nowadays, as sober granddads, they are accusing their grand-children, what with their smoking pot, wearing bikinis, their miniskirts and hair, of going to hell on a rollercoaster.

There was a story told of the last legal hanging in Camden, with the inevitable group of curious spectators present, when the prisoner, his neck unbroken by the fall through the trap door, refused to die. After considerable gyration by the hap-less victim, the jailer, acting as executioner, was forced to grab the condemned man by the heels and add his weight to that of the victim's before his neck was, mercifully, broken.

There were real and ugly stories, as well as others vague and whispered, of Reconstruction days. How the Yankees who came down as settlers after the war were not only threatened with violence but shot at, one coming out alive but with several bullet holes in his clothing; how these Yankees were treated with derision and contempt; how Negroes were intimidated or beaten to prevent them from voting or getting out of hand; how some, bolder than others, were found hanging inside covered bridges—gruesome warnings to others—or were sent on nice "quiet trips" to Mobile via the Alabama River; how ballot boxes were stuffed and, after the votes were counted, destroyed, until the county government was finally wrested from the Negroes and Yankees and returned to the control of the native whites.

Other bizarre stories, about strange people who did outlandish things, that traveled across the river to be told over our dining table or in the haze of tobacco smoke before winter fires, also left disturbing memories. There was the incident of a prominent citizen who killed another over the price of a turkey. There was the egotist who boasted of picking out his third wife at the graveside of his second and declaring after a whirlwind courtship and third marriage that a wife was like a piece of furniture—a handy thing to have about the place. There was the incredible tale of an overly pious citizen who, when his son drowned in the river after disobeying him by going swimming on the Sabbath, declared he would not grieve for the boy, since he was without doubt being punished by the Lord for the double sin of disobedience and of not keeping the Sabbath holy. Affirming his conviction, this fanatical father attended church and sang and prayed with gusto on the very day of the tragedy. Also this same man was said to have caught his neighbor's hogs, which were rooting up his garden, and while singing "Jesus Lover of my Soul," gouged their eyes out before releasing them.

It was not hearsay but fact that at times in the past, congregations in Camden had turned people out of their churches for what the ruling authorities considered sins of sufficient enormity. One such case was that of a young lady from a "best" family who was "churched" for bodily contact in dancing; another, an officer, churched for traveling on Sunday; another for publicly imbibing too freely. Even though these offenders were eventually reinstated after prayer, repentance, and forgiveness, such incidents conjured up in my young mind pictures of unduly severe church censure meted out by authorities whom I presumed were less than perfect themselves, and might have better heeded the Lord's admonition, "Judge not, that ye be not judged."

A matter that concerned me even more vitally than church discipline, however, was that imposed by school authorities on teachers. Teachers were reported to have been spied upon by trustees and principals and were subject to dismissal for such "questionable" conduct as dating on school nights or smoking, even in private, or taking a drink anywhere, or being seen in certain company or in certain places. As a new teacher and something of a stranger, how was I to know the who, what, and where of all these taboos?

Waves of gossip and scandal, news of fights and feuds and killings, after surging over the community, and eventually drifting over the county, had left me with a feeling of apprehension about this place of my destination. Fortunately, each wave of unhappy news lasted only until another and more fascinating obliterated it. As someone caught in one of these onslaughts remarked, "Would that some other poor devil would foul up so as to get the hounds off my trail."

There was, as was apt to be in any county seat, the occasional killing of a law officer by a Negro or of a defiant Negro by an officer; the shooting of a white citizen by another white or of a Negro by a white if the Negro was thought to have murdered someone or attempted rape. Such tragedies left wounds of tension and anger that were long in healing.

Yet with all these unhappy reflections there were instances of graciousness, gallantry, and excellence that I might better have thought upon: how those daredevils had gone off to colleges and universities and had become outstanding doctors, lawyers, judges, professors, and statesmen, some returning to their hometown, others settling in more populous places; how men and women, disdaining hand-outs, cared for their own in illness, bereavement, in loss of home or business, through fires, floods and depression. No one went begging, no one went unloved or unnoticed. Friends helped nurse each other's sick, doctors spent days and nights at bedsides of patients and rode miles on horseback to attend them, purses were taken up for distress victims, both black and white; no man was a Rockefeller, but no man suffered from want or was buried in a pauper's grave.

Besides the taken-for-granted gallantry to women, there were accounts of man-to-man gallantry in these old families, even in their indiscretions and excesses. If such a one became embroiled in a fight, friends and neighbors pitched in with fists or pistols to assist the underdog; if he got drunk, he was taken

home and tenderly cared for until sober; if he lost at horseracing or chicken-fighting or poker playing, he paid his debts if
possible; if not possible, his I.O.U. was destroyed and the debt
forgiven.

There was much more I would learn about my destination,
and it would be both gratifying and surprising. But at this
moment of transition, whatever doubts I had could not silence
the hope in my heart.

FIVE

The Town Itself

Many of the antebellum homes of Canton Bend and adjoining
'Possum Bend have gone by fire or fallen into ruin. But a few
remain: the Marsh Tait home—which was spared by the Yankees in the last gasp of the war in exchange for the contents of a
well-stocked wine cellar—the Ervin's, the Harris's, the Starr's,
and the Smith's. In Camden proper remain the Beck home,
restored by the Darwins who now live there; the McWilliams'
home, now the Shook residence, and others of lesser age and
beauty. But so close are the family ties and the interdepen-
dence of town and plantation that Camden claims them all.

By whatever road one enters Camden, one does not see
many of these old homes. Entering by Canton Drive, as I did
that September day, one would not be impressed by what he
saw. From the appearance of homes on this residential street,
Camden might have been any one of many small towns of the
Black Belt; unpretentious clapboarded houses, once white,
green-shuttered, set inside white paling or iron fences; a few
old colonial houses with imposing columns, balconies and
peeling paint, set far back behind ancient magnolias, water
oaks and gnarled crepe myrtle; tumble-down houses held
together by iron-sinewed wisteria vines; rambling, added-on-
to houses with gingerbread trim and rusty tin roofing overlay-
ing old wood shingles—the tin glaring inharmoniously above

the simple weatherboarded bodies. No brick homes. Not a one. Beside most houses were fenced-in garden plots and behind most were barns for milch cows and horses, while nondescript servants' houses stood somewhere in the background.

Going down Canton Drive, I realized I was leaving the residential area when the churches, two with steeples and belfries, two without, began to appear. Four churches, all Protestant, in calling distance of each other—all pointing the identical way to Heaven, but set apart because, long ago, interpreters of the Scripture fell to hair-splitting and could not agree on such matters as sprinkling versus immersion, backsliding versus falling from grace, and the singing of hymns versus the singing of psalms.

Close by the churches stood the elementary and high-school buildings for white children, one a simple wooden building, the other old brick with white columns, weather-worn, child-abused; which, however, before the day of public schools was the proud Camden Female Institute, where were taught the things a cultured southern lady of the 1800s should know— Latin, Greek, piano, music (both instrumental and vocal), picture painting, dramatics, elocution, and etiquette.

Across the road lay the cemetery, enclosed by an iron fence and dominated by the inevitable monument to the Civil War dead—a forlorn soldier atop the traditional marble shaft, leaning on his rifle, brooding not only over his own lost cause but possibly over other causes his proud and stubborn descendants have lost and must yet lose.

A story about this old monument came to mind as I passed that way—remembered perhaps because it seemed such an impish proof of what time and nature can do to man's idols. Memorial services for the Civil War dead were (and still are), weather permitting, held at the base of this monument. Originally there was an old cannon nearby (what became of it no one seems to know) and the plan, for a particular U.D.C. commemorative service, was to fire the old field piece as a grand finale to the eulogies for the heroic dead and pledges that the living should never forget. After a stirring speech by an orator of no small renown, the charge—minus the cannon ball, of course—was ignited. The spectators held hands over ears and squeezed eyes shut in anticipation of the blast to follow. Alas! Only a poor "poof" and a small wisp of smoke came from the mouth of the old monster. At that particular moment, as if to add insult to deflation, a bird, which had taken a rest on the cap of the old marble soldier, disturbed from his reverie, flew up and carelessly dropped his autograph onto the bare head of the hapless speaker.

Past the Masonic Hall and the business area tumbled into view. Here most of the structures were brick, old and faded, some made by slaves, some mellow with time and others speckled with peeling paint. The exposed side of one of the largest buildings was only half-painted, as if the painter had dropped dead on the job. I later came to know what happened to that building. The painter, Jack Tepper, was a kinsman of the famous English artist William Turner. Jack was in the process of painting this building when he heard that he had inherited a portion of the fortune left by the great Turner. Immediately he dropped bucket and brush, descended the scaffolding, and declared that he'd never paint another house as long as he lived. The long unpainted half of the wall bore evidence that he had meant what he said.

A large brick structure, set in a tree-shaded square, immediately identified Camden as a county seat, for the building was unmistakably the courthouse. With its large, fluted Corinthian columns and its twin, wrought-iron stairway across the front and leading to the upper story, this building not only dominated the little town but lent it dignity and poise. The structure, built by Sandy Bragg in 1857, was well-proportioned, balanced, graceful, yet massive.

Benches under the trees were lined with behatted farmers, their faces brown and seamed like walnut hulls and their eyes squinting through gold-rimmed spectacles, chewing cheroots or plug tobacco, paring fingernails with whittling knives, and swapping comments, no doubt, about the durn gov'ment, the "dry" drought, po' crops, and fool taxes. A grayish, powdery dust, pounded out by a thousand hooves and wheels, churned up by passing cars, hung in a gauzy veil over the courthouse square and drifted into the jumble of business houses clustered around it.

From the clots of Negroes sitting on the sleek, whittled-on street benches and standing idle on street corners, there was no mistaking the day of the week. It was Saturday afternoon— "Saddy" to the Negroes—the traditional day off for them to come to town, afoot, muleback, or sitting in straight, split-bottomed chairs placed in wagon bodies, to get their weekly rations, to see friends and families, to drink soda pop (if one had a nickle to spare), to listen to the jukebox on the back street, to laugh and joree each other, while babies slept fitfully in their mothers' laps and dined often at bared breasts.

But instead of the usual banter and lusty backslapping among them, there was a listless quietude. Looking like scarecrows in their patched and repatched clothes, either barefoot or with shoes made of pieces of inner tubes tied together with string, arms drooping like leaves on a withering plant, these benighted humans were the trailing end of a Great Depression begun for them long before others knew its effects. Like a relentless winepress, it had squeezed the easy laughter from their hearts and the last few pennies from their pockets.

And because the Negroes had no money for trading, merchants stood idly in the doors of their stores, which bounded the courthouse square like a child's uneven, multicolored building blocks piled haphazardly around a central fort. The sidewalks, dirt here, concrete there, jumped up, worn down, paper-littered, shaded in spots by a sort of awning made of corrugated tin roofing, offered access to these buildings, whose fly-specked windows were plastered with advertisements of Cardui, Garrett's Sweet Snuff, Lydia E. Pinkham's Compound, and Brown Mule's Chewing Tobacco.

Inside, if one looked closely, tables of merchandise covered with muslin could be seen, looking as if someone had drawn sheets up over the dead—actually only partial protection from the dust. Long strips of flypaper hung from the ceilings, puny traps for that pesky insect whose propagation in uncollected garbage and open privies went unhindered. Attached to strings, also hanging from the ceilings, like stalactites in a cave, were articles of clothing—from black cotton stockings, bloomers, and bandanas, to overalls, sunhats, and broghans. Farther back, from sturdy hooks, hung trace chains, plow-points, saddle blankets, and split-bottomed chairs. Big potbel-lied stoves with oversized sandboxes around them for catching burnt matches, tobacco spittle, and tobacco "chaws," stood bleak and black in the middle of most of the stores. But come winter and these old iron hulks, glowing with flame and belch-ing fumes, would draw people, whether customers or not, in from the streets as a magnet draws steel filings from a carpen-ter's bench.

Though cluttered and unkempt, this was the way country folks liked their goods displayed. Fix up a store neat and orderly and they would consider it citified and shun it like the plague.

In the road and on the sidewalks, everywhere, stretched out sunning themselves or sitting nonchalantly scratching them-selves, were dogs. Dozens of them. Lank and mangy, fat and sleek. Long-eared fox hounds—Walkers, Blue Ticks, Red Bones, and potlickers—setters, pointers, and mongrels with corkscrew tails and feisty faces. But no lap dogs and none on leashes. (Anyone leading a dog on a leash would have been marked as a stranger and a suspect one at that.) People stepped over them or walked around them, cars drove around those stretched out in the street as if dead. Some were patted on the head and spoken to as if they were people—all treated like the sacred bulls of India.

I wondered why people in the midst of such privation would or could feed so many dogs. But, as hunting season came along, I understood. Hunting—fox, quail, turkey, deer—was the king's sport for the white man; rabbit, coon, squirrel, 'possum, for the Negro living in the backcountry, a necessity.

His dog, gun, stick, and fishing pole enabled him to supplement his streak-o'-fat and streak-o'-lean diet and hold body and soul together until the Good Lord decided to part them.

At corners, angles, or in the middle of everything sat knobby cedar poles plastered with pictures of last year's political candidates, strung with frazzled light lines and drooping telephone wires from which hung wisps of straw and string, remnants of last year's sparrow nests and boys' abandoned kites.

There were other parts of town I would learn about later. But it was now sundown. Refreshed by a coke, I bought some groceries and continued on to my new abode. And I was lucky. I had obtained an apartment close to school with people who, I had been assured, were quality folks. My new home consisted of a bedroom and sitting room combined, a kitchenette with a two-burner oil stove for cooking, and a share-the-bath in the rear of the house—all for the huge amount of $7.50 a month. Deducting this from my promised salary of $85.00 a month, I would have $77.50 left. Eight months of this, if school lasted that long, must pay my debts and provide food, clothes, and doctoring for myself and my eight-year-old son for a whole year. It would take some doing. But it must suffice.

It was not an auspicious beginning. But, when I spread sheets on the bare mattress that evening and a cloth on the kitchen table, a sort of glow warmed my heart. For some unreasonable reason I felt as snug as a cricket on a warm winter hearth.

SIX

People with a Past

Like many Deep South towns, Camden is both blessed and burdened with a past. Blessed because of a goodly heritage that the past has bestowed upon it, burdened because much of the past is painful and will not die. High on the list of reasons for Camden's being what it is, is its loyalty to, its admiration for, and its real sense of continuity with the past. The roots of the people are here, their history is here, their grandparents and great-grandparents lie in the public cemetery or in small private, iron-fenced plots near old home sites. Names of families are old names, people are known not just for themselves but are what they are because their forebears were thus and so.

Camden is what it is also because it is a child of the often romanticized, often vilified, Black Belt country. This swatch of land, stretching from central Mississippi across south central Alabama, received its name not, as is often thought, from the predominance of Negroes within its bounds, but from its soil, which ranges from creepy, tar-black prairie—as sticky as chewing gum when wet, as crumbly as meal when dry—to mixtures of the black soil with clays, limes, and sandy loams.

Much of this soil, once as rich as a hen-house floor, which attracted early settlers to stop and stay, was by the year 1933 lying on the bottom of the Gulf of Mexico. Pastures had been overgrazed, timberlands overcut, farms overcultivated, with little effort to conserve what was left or replenish what had been lost. But out of the harsh Depression years would come one of the few welcome government programs of soil conservation and rehabilitation; so welcome that in the span of half a lifetime the Black Belt would again become a chosen spot for God's green thumb.

The Black Belt country's history, though on a more modest scale, resembles that of the Mississippi Delta. Like the Delta it was excellent cotton country. Through it flowed accessible navigable streams, while the growing of cotton was an occupation suited to the slaves' abilities and inclinations. The combination of soil, climate, and slavery added up to a modest sort of gone-with-the-wind life that, during antebellum days, was stable and in most respects worthy. If its greatest support and at the same time its greatest defect was slavery, this defect by the time of the Civil War was becoming an insupportable burden—so much so that had the war not freed the slaves, costs of feeding, clothing, and caring for them would have in time done so. (Not that "in time" would have been soon enough.)

Since most of the white families of the Black Belt are reputedly descendants of these old landed families, probably the most coveted legacy the past has bestowed on it and concurrently on the inhabitants of Camden is the caliber of its people. They were in the early days, and still are, to a great degree, quality folks. (Just how quality folks come by this distinction is a hotly disputed issue, but if not inherited, it without doubt takes some generations to acquire.)

These white immigrants did not become quality folk because of their affluence in the antebellum system, though it may have afforded the means and adornments to set them off to advantage. They were quality folk because they came from quality folk; staunch, freedom-loving, high-minded pioneer stock, largely from Virginia and the Carolinas, of English and Scottish descent, interested in improving their economic status to be sure, but also in the cultural areas of life—religion, learning, arts and letters, and refinement of the social graces. No wonder that, with affluence, these people blossomed into a sort of aristocracy, faintly mirroring the baronial life in the old countries whence they came—a life that placed good living above the exigencies of making a living.

However, the Black Belt aristocracy differed from that of the old countries in that it represented not an old and established way of life, but only a thin, fragile veneer, that never quite concealed the tough, brawling pioneer who hewed his first domain from the raw forest with his own hands, whose first house was built of logs, and who had little education and few graces.

Of course, some pioneers were rascals: land prospectors, fugitives from justice, slave traders, Indian fighters, hard-drinking and loose-living people. But most of them were drifters who did not stay and put down roots. Certainly they were in the minority and their influence was not profound. Not that some of the quality folk weren't high livers and hell raisers too, but there was a difference, as between a common highwayman and a Robin Hood.

In spite of their Calvinistic leanings, these antebellum forefathers loved their horse racing, fox hunting, cock fighting, dueling, poker playing, and liquor drinking; while their feminine companions indulged in gentler pastimes, such as embroidering pillow shams, painting fruit and flower pictures, making wedding-ring quilts, playing the piano, writing verse, and keeping diaries. Both sexes lightened their lives with much visiting, sometimes for days, sometimes for months, and by dining, dancing, and "vocalizing." With slaves to relieve them of onerous duties, they could afford to indulge in such niceties.

When the Civil War left these ladies and gentlemen as bereft of their accoutrements as chickens plucked by a cyclone, a few succumbed to an early demise, or gave up their lands for taxes, or folded up and left the country. But others survived, with their courage, pride, good manners, and bare lands—nothing more. Bereft as they were, however, they bequeathed to their descendants the social habits and manners that make life here meaningful and pleasant. I daresay that no other people in North America work harder at upholding the amenities of life and less arduously at the business of making a living; with the result that, through bleak days and balmy, they get more fun and satisfaction than most people out of the grim grind of life.

Because their great-grandparents had doted on education, many sending their children abroad for advanced study, because their grandparents were of the same mind, even though they were probably denied instruction beyond that afforded by a one or two-room school, the present generation of old Black Belt families would sell their souls, though not their land, to educate their children properly. And great are the lamentations and shame should the offspring (if able) prove unwilling to get a college education.

Yet there is a strange paradox here. Anyone letting his erudition show in speech or an avant-garde manner is suspect and is branded, good naturedly, as an educated fool. High-flown oratory and verbose rhetoric were "back there" considered enviable accomplishments, especially from politicians and preachers; but in later years the politician, realizing the voting power of the common man, shucked coat, collar, tie, sometimes even shoes, and waded into the English language with a meat cleaver.

Governor "Big Jim" Folsom, with his suds bucket to clean out that crowd of rascals in Montgomery, knew what he was doing when he told his audiences here in the Black Belt: "Sho I stole frum those big mules in Birmingham and give it to you po' folks down here. I did it befo', and I'll do it again. See that Cadillac I ride 'round in? Well, it's yore's. Come up to Montgomery and I'll take you 'round in it and feed you some turnip greens and pot-liquor in yore own mansion up there, Ya'll come!" The house would come down with applause and Folsom went in for a third term.

Sadly for the Black Belt, art, drama, ballet, poetry, writing (to a degree), all the arts except playing and singing which were acceptable as feminine accomplishments, have been so neglected, except as private hobbies, that our artistic abilities have long lain latent and unmined. Fortunately, the winds have at last changed. Our young men are now permitted to choose careers of music or art with genuine approval of their elders, and girls study whatever their hearts desire.

Because, to their ancestors, children were a blessing and joy, present Black Belt parents dote on their children to the point of maudlin sentimentality. Loved and spoiled, these children, regardless of what the psychology books may say, turn out better than most, and in turn humor their elders and put up with them even into cranky and cantankerous old age.

Looking back through an aura of time and wistful imaginings, most white Black Belters sincerely believe that their antebellum ancestors owned thousands of acres of land and hundreds of slaves. The fact is that very few were so well off. Most had no slaves at all. Others only a few. But the idea is more powerful than the truth. Through the years it has allowed the not-so-well-off to blame the War and Reconstruction for the loss of family fortunes, whether such fortunes ever existed or not; and it has imbued sons and grandsons with a passion to acquire land, the family's lost land perhaps, or simply land. Or with retaining land bequeathed to them. Sell land? Never! In the past, land meant power and prestige in the Black Belt; today it may be no more than a badge of wealth, but the badge bears a sort of regal connotation nonetheless.

Because a man's religion and morals were molded in the old days to suit his circumstances and convenience, these areas of life are still considered a man's own particular business, and few be the ministers of the gospel who attempt to change them. Clerics and church organizations that meddle in politics and social reform, doctrines that deviate from the infallibility of the Scripture—though all men decipher them differently—or any new-fangled notion concerning form or ritual or the congregation's comfort in the pew, are anathema to Black Belt Protestants. But believe in the power of Almighty God they do.

Religion is powerful, but politics is an axe with a handle to it that people can lay hands on. White Black Belters would never admit that they got themselves into a war they couldn't win because of earlier political defeats, but they have never forgotten that they won the War of Reconstruction at the ballot box. Such Black Belters still enjoy the blood and heat of the political cockpit, even though many do not stir themselves to go to the polls on voting day. And when they do go they oftener vote "agin sump'en" than "fer sump'en."

There are a number of mavericks and unluckies in this group of white quality folk of the Black Belt. They come from just as good families, often the very same families. They may not own much land; they are likely to be small farmers, artisans, or tradesmen, and they are, to their everlasting credit, less dependent on some nebulous past for their ways of thinking and acting. Though they may or may not be able to hark back to some illustrious family history, they couldn't care less. Though they could probably climb their family trees back to as

famous a D.A.R. or Colonial Dame limb as another, they don't
give a whoop in Hades about such bunk. They'll tell you quick
enough that, in digging up family skeletons, one is as apt to dig

up a Jesse James or a Rube Burrows as a George Washington
or a Robert E. Lee.

These people may not have a college education, but they
have a knowledge of hounds, coons, deer, turkey, fishing, the
weather, crops, and gov'ment shenanigans that would con-
found Confucius. And if anything, they are prouder and more
hardheaded than those who can trace their families back to
kings and queens. They dang-well know what they know, and
they aren't handcuffed by parlor manners or this *noblesse oblige*
stuff in saying so. They may act on hunches and plant by the
almanac, but their company is sought after, particularly on the
benches around the courthouse and on hunting and fishing
expeditions. And each of their votes is worth as much as the
lord of creation's; and if they want these voters, politicians
must dance to their fiddle.

In its heyday, when the Black Belt was the wealthiest and
most populous part of the state, it gained a place of power and
prominence in the state's political life far beyond its size. Until
recent years the Black Belt counties had one senator per
county while two or three counties in other parts of the state
shared one. But, although population and wealth shifted, the
conservative, segregationist Black Belt senators, stubbornly
guarding the status quo, refused for sixty-five years to do what
the state constitution of 1901 decreed, reapportion the state
every ten years. Hence the Black Belt retained its power over
state government until the federal courts ordered Alabama to
reapportion itself, applying the one-man, one-vote rule. Consequently, to a degree greater than would seem possible, the
stamp and reflection of the Black Belt have, through the years,
marked the stance of our state in affairs at home and abroad.

Now the balance of power is weighted in favor of the more
heavily industrialized counties and big cities, most of which,
with the exception of Montgomery and Mobile, are in the
northern part of the state. Relinquishing power to the north-

ern counties and city slickers was almost as humiliating to the Black Belt as relinquishing power to the Yankees in the 1860s; but perhaps all is not lost. Perchance, with factories now lighting down in our cotton patches and piney woods, we may become city slickers ourselves and join these lucky rascals.

In wake of the Civil War, Negroes in the Black Belt barely made do in a labor market cheapened by their great numbers. During the Great Depression, when I came to Camden, they were hardly as well off in material things as when they were cared for by masters. Even their landlords were no longer able to help them as much as their paternalistic instincts dictated. They, too, were poor. Poor as Job's turkey. But the blacks were poorer and more helpless. And there were so many, many more of them.

SEVEN

Marking the Shoals

Because my father was born here and here had friends of long standing, because one pair of grandparents and one of great-grandparents had lived and died here, because this Camden grandfather fought in the Civil War, and because I had an older sister who had lived here for twenty years, I felt that I held a sort of key to Camden. I was not a stranger. In this I was fortunate.

Feeling welcome and accepted, I might have fallen into an attitude of complacency, perhaps carelessness, had not my older sister soon paid me a visit and given me a briefing on some of the pitfalls that, with a false step or two on my part, might endanger or undo all this ready-made goodwill.

Mamie was the oldest of nine children; I was next to the youngest. Being eighteen years my senior, she was well qualified to give me advice. Fortunately I had arrived at a certain milepost up fool's hill where I was at least willing to listen.

After all, I hadn't done too well following my own compass. But a frank discussion of my situation and the admonition I was about to receive turned out to be something like applying soap and suds to a housecat.

Taking her church work quite seriously, Mamie began by putting first things first, "I married into the Methodist Church," she began, "but you are still Presbyterian. So I suggest that you go to your own church and go regularly. Then join it as soon as you are invited to do so. You'll want to do whatever church work you can. Teach a Sunday School Class if you are asked," she continued, "join the Missionary Society, and go to prayer meetings and Bible study if possible."

That sounded like a sizable order. Although I had been derelict about going to church regularly in recent years, mainly because of the rebellion in my twenties against fundamentalism, I was not unwilling to return. I had already decided that my rebellion was not against the church itself, but only against some theological hieroglyphics on the church's wall. But, willing or unwilling, I knew my sister's advice was wise. Church affiliation was one requisite for a schoolteacher's acceptance. Hence there was no argument here.

"You will probably be asked to join a women's club," Mamie continued, "and in due time you should do so. In this way you will meet women outside your church and school. And whatever you do, return all your social calls promptly. Keep a list and don't miss anyone." Then after a pause—"If you haven't done so already, I'll get your papers in order and apply for your D.A.R. and U.D.C. memberships."

About this last suggestion I remonstrated weakly. At the time I had little enthusiasm for women's organizations, which seemed to do more talking and eating than working, and I wondered whether the United Daughters of the Confederacy weren't keeping alive many unhappy memories that might best be forgot. Also, probably from cartoons and caricatures, I had acquired the notion that the Daughters of the American Revolution were a group of prim, lavender-and-old-lace ladies, making speeches, waving flags, and marching backward, just as I had pictured a suffragette as a mannish, hatchet-faced woman and a W.C.T.Uer as a pious, square-toed do-gooder. (But I was younger then, afflicted with a lot of rebellious idealism, with no idea that with age I would come to admire, if not revere, the wonder and wisdom of the past.) But since my mother, sisters, and older kin were members of these patriotic organizations, and since my children and grandchildren might someday cherish affiliation with them, certainly I should not be the broken link in the chain. Thus I deferred to my sister's better judgment.

Then, over a cup of tea set out on the kitchen table, Mamie began to speak to me of other matters, which concerned her more acutely. Since her husband had been principal of the Camden High School at one time—and a darned good one by the standards of the day, strong for discipline and hard work and hard on dawdling and monkeyshines—and since her children had attended the same school, she spoke with authority.

"I hate to remind you," she began apologetically, "but you realize, of course, that you came here under a cloud."

She waited a moment for me to get my bearings. My sins began to parade themselves before me like accusing ghosts.

Then Mamie folded her hands and sighed sadly. "What a pity," she said, "that you couldn't have been a sod widow instead of a grass one."

Would I never be through with this unhappy chapter in my life? But why was a grass widow considered so tarnished and suspect while a sod widow was thought of as crystal pure? Accusations and defenses tumbled over themselves in my brain until one fell out on the absurd side. "Next time," I suggested, "I'll put a spider in his dumpling."

"If there is a next time," my sister warned me.

Then while I tried to gain my equilibrium I was told: "Absolutely no drinking, no smoking." Although she was just "telling me for my own good," I had a feeling that it was also in hopes of preserving her pride and peace of mind. And finally, what I had feared. "You may in time be asked for a date. Widows are fair bait, you know. And you must not go out with the wrong person."

"But how am I to know?" I ventured.

"Clear it with me," my guardian angel answered. "But," she added reluctantly, "I must tell you that there are only two or three eligible men hereabouts of the proper age for you to see in this capacity."

"Two or three?" I repeated incredulously, considering this bleak prospect for my future.

"One never knows," sighed Mamie again. "Maybe the Lord will lend a hand. Sometimes He works in strange and mysterious ways."

It did appear that I was going to need some help from above, or I'd be grounded for my stay in Camden. The trouble was, I was not accustomed to allowing Providence to solve my problems. I had not even allowed my elders to help solve them, and I was in for some sort of reformation to adjust to such a supine approach to a problem. I believed that the Lord helped those who helped themselves. It wouldn't be easy to sit by and hope for a miracle such as we were discussing. This would take some thinking on.

Although I knew that these suggestions were offered in love and for my own good, they reinforced my feeling of unease about Camden. I could only wish that another drove of stars would fall on Alabama or the sun would decide to turn around and rise in the West so as to divert the attention of these good people away from me and my painful plight.

However, if my chances of going out with a member of the opposite sex were so nearly nil, prospects of my being indiscreet would apparently be reduced to a minimum. Under these circumstances there should be little cause for concern. A lone school teacher sitting at home nights grading papers could hardly create a gossipy situation. Nevertheless, a bleak, lonely feeling cast a chill over my enthusiasm for this step I was taking into the unknown.

"One other thing," Mamie added as if, happily, she was on

the last lap of this unpleasant duty of having to tell it like it was, "You must above all things make the school children behave, never let them get out of hand. People here have never forgotten how a few years ago the big boys in the high school got the upper hand of the principal, a Mr. Moore, a fine Christian gentleman if there ever was one, and made a shambles of the school. It took Professor Hardy to straighten things out. Never was there such a man for such a moment as Mr. Hardy," she declared, breaking out in sunshine all over.

I was more than glad to switch the conversation from my liabilities to the epic reign of Professor Hardy in the Camden High School. Though I had heard much about him and would never hear the last of this real-life hero, I encouraged my sister to fill in the details for me.

It seems that Professor Moore had come to Camden from a much smaller school where he had been held in the highest esteem. But he stepped into the Camden school at a critical juncture, during the hip-flask and bobbed-hair, flapper days, when law and order were being flouted by the high school boys to such an extent that they were on the verge of open rebellion. These boys, from the moment Mr. Moore arrived, decided, like Joshua, to spy out the land, and in their early skirmishes discovered that the reasoning, counseling, powder-puff discipline of the new principal was a pushover for their tactics. They reacted to his moralizing by laughing in his face, they refused to stay in after school, they refused to be whipped, and would not stay home if expelled.

They overturned the men's privy, once with one of the teachers locked inside, put firecrackers and cartridges in the potbellied stoves, stuffed the jointed stovepipes with rags, or pulled them apart, put Epsom salts in the drinking water, released live rats, birds, lizards, snakes in the classrooms, came to classes late or not at all, played hooky when they pleased, tore up the town on Halloween, broke up the school dances, and generally perpetrated all the deviltry their brains could concoct.

After one year of this, Mr. Moore had had it, so to speak, as principal, and he gladly shook the dust off his pedagogical feet, never to return to Camden in such capacity again. But by this time the parents had also lost control and were helplessly wringing their hands over their defiant offspring. In such a state of affairs the board of education went searching for a principal who might be able to control such an insurrection. But finding someone willing to put his head into this hornet's nest was not easy.

After many conferences with prospects, the board came upon a man, a Mr. Claude Hardy, highly recommended as a strong disciplinarian, who, they decided, might fill the bill. But with Mr. Hardy the board found all precedents for hiring a teacher reversed. Instead of their telling him what he was to do, he gave them a mandate telling them and all parents that he would take the school only if given absolute authority over his charges and only if parents backed him up in whatever discipline he meted out.

In desperation the board and parents agreed to go along with this proposal. Fortunately, Professor Hardy proved to be the Jack Dempsey for this critical crunch—tough sinewed, tough talking, wise in the ways of erring young flesh, decisive, unrelenting, and not afraid of the devil himself. But withal he was a scholar, and demanded and got scholarly effort from both teachers and pupils. His edicts for both teachers and pupils covered all their activities, on duty and off. No child was to be seen on the downtown streets of Camden at any time without a pass or a written excuse from his parents; no student or teacher was to have a date during the five-day school week; no dancing, card playing, pool shooting or night riding whatever, either by students or teachers; no infraction of a hundred rules of conduct on the school grounds.

His punishment for the boys for disobedience was a belting, one laid on with a will, and if there was any objection he would take on the offender in a bare-fist fight and summarily knock hell out of him. For lesser pranks and for female offenders he used milder correction: staying after school, for an hour or a month of hours, depending on the gravity of the offense;

standing on one foot by the half hour, holding a heavy dictionary out at arm's length for ten minutes, bending fingers backward, lifting out of seats by the hair or ears, or canceling weekend date or town privileges.

Furthermore, he delegated to no one his business of sleuth, judge, and jury. He stayed on duty, on campus and off, for eighteen hours a day; and the boys, who are now gray-headed men, swear that he had a pair of eyes in the back of his head and slept with these two open. But his tactics brought results. Fighting fire with fire, he so effectively instilled respect for law and order into this group of youngsters that in after years they came to hold up Professor Hardy as a hero, and they themselves grew into such circumspect and conventional behavior that many of them in due time became elders, deacons, school trustees, officers of the law, and doctors of the law or of medicine.

In retrospect it is interesting to note that these once obstreperous boys and their once-flapper wives—some of whom first learned back in those days to drink and smoke like men—who invented the bunny-hug and cheek-to-cheek dancing, were later shocked out of their minds by their boogie-woogieing, bobby-soxed, zoot-suited, rocking-and-rolling children; who now in their mellow years are fairly thrown into strokes or obituary columns by their miniclad, hirsute, cohabiting, drug-tampering, streaking grandchildren. Maybe these oldtimers should remember the pebbles they dropped into the pool when they were young.

Though it was on a happier note that my sister departed, I still was aware that, whether taken seriously or in good humor, Professor Hardy's example was one still held in high esteem by patrons of the Camden school. And sadly for me, making people behave themselves, even kids, even myself, was not my particular forte.

Other matters and other people were discussed at other times. "Watch out for the gossipy tongue of so-and-so," Mamie would warn me. "Be careful what you say. Best keep your mouth shut. Don't become involved in an argument, especially about politics or religion. Remember that this person doesn't speak to that person—ancient grudge over land-lines, an unpaid debt, or something no one now recalls. That family is the salt of the earth, even if poor as gully dirt; this family won't do; not our kind of folks. Never invite this one without inviting that. They're inseparable. Never criticize anybody until you know everybody; you'd likely be talking to a sister, aunt, or cousin."

My sister's advice survived her by many years, and it was tested and proven wise beyond compare, especially when I failed to follow it.

EIGHT

The Name of the Game

The name of the game is the same, fifty years ago, twenty-five, today. Call it education, if you can or must; but clumsily, gropingly, it lumbers along, always overloaded, underpowered, creaking a generation behind the winged monster of progress. But in spite of the state of the grinding stones, out of the old mill come young people, about the same in every day and age: some who have learned and would have learned under any circumstances, some who can never learn, and others who forever "goof off" and learn as little as possible.

In the year of '33, schools all over Alabama were stuck on the bottom of a bone-dry well. Most teachers were paid by warrants, most schools running five to seven months unless subsidized by local patrons to pay the teachers for a longer term. There was no money for janitor service, P.T.A.s were paying light bills and buying coal, chalk, and toilet paper; things that wore out simply fell apart or were done without. Not that the children minded. They sensed such privations not at all and were delighted when schools closed in March instead of May. And the teachers, not finding anything else to do, were satisfied to teach for seventy-five or eighty dollars a month and that paid in warrants, which were rarely redeemable in cash, whatever the discount offered. Fortunately, merchants took them in for food and clothing, and the teachers survived, though not very handily.

Consequently, I felt lucky to have a job in any school, but particularly in the principal high school in the county, one that had so far progressed as to have a teacher for each grade, inside toilets (even if they worked only by fits and spells), drinking fountains (even if they furnished only tepid water), and modern additions of home economics and vocational agriculture to the basic curriculum. Like the children, I did not feel deprived or imposed upon by having to teach in this rather Spartan environment. After all, it had considerably more to recommend it than that in which I had received my schooling a few short years before. By comparison I had landed in quite an up-to-date school.

My childhood school in the same county boasted two rooms—one upstairs, one down—and two teachers. The six primary grades were taught by a woman, usually an old maid, while the high school was taught by a man, the principal, always with impeccable recommendations, and usually of considerable ability.

In my youth all students within crow-flying distance of school walked there and back twice daily, going all the way home for their noontime meal. We walked those several miles, rain or shine, sun or sleet, for the very simple reason that there was no way to get ourselves fetched back and forth. I do not recall feeling persecuted in having to make these journeys, but I do recall enjoying the many dilly-dallyings along the way— wading in the branch, picking primroses, plums, or dewberries, gathering hickory nuts and scaly-barks, hopping onto backs of wagons, or rushing to the railroad crossing when the yellow banana car hove into view so as to get the overripe bananas thrown to us by the freightman. I am thankful that we were never told that these daily treks were a boon to our health, for had we been told, we would have found a great deal less pleasure in them.

Pupils who lived too far away from school to walk, rode mule-back or in some contrivance with wheels. These children brought their dinners in buckets with lids that came off at a mighty pull on rings in their tops; on cold, rainy days we foot-pupils envied them their cold sweet potatoes and biscuits soaked in sorghum syrup.

Though we had no "crip" courses and no frills to relieve us from the book, tablet, slate and dictionary, we managed nevertheless to cover the essentials that qualified us for entrance to colleges of our choice. If one did not make his grades he was, not cruelly, but mercifully, refused graduation. We had no diplomas, no caps or gowns, no long-winded speeches to denote this milestone in our lives. School just joyously closed, without one dance, speech, or tear; the nongraduates free with their dignity intact, along with the rest.

Teachers held continuous recitations while students not reciting were supposed to study at their desks. There was no such thing as a study hall. But we were no more addicted to studying than children are nowadays; rather we spent most of this valuable time making spitballs—the ceiling looked like a barnacled ship bottom so plastered was it with these missiles—whittling on our desks, writing love notes, or drawing hate pictures.

Happily, recitations lasted from fifteen to thirty minutes, a time span about as long as a child's mind can be hitched in one spot. The idea that a pupil's recitation period last an hour must have been made by his elders in propitiation for their guilt in not being able to listen to their preachers for longer than twenty minutes at a stretch. Anyway, we learned a lot that way.

Probably because these teachers considered a child's advancement as a reflection of their abilities, they were willing to work as hard at imparting knowledge as they expected their charges to work at acquiring it. They knew about "slow learners"—heaven knows they had enough of them—but they worked under the assumption that every child could learn if he tried hard enough and kept at it long enough. Consequently, they inflicted on themselves the same punishment inflicted on the dullard or the laggard by staying in after school until the lesson of the day was learned. This after-school tutoring was limited only by the hours of the day. If the benighted one did not master his lesson sooner, he was not set free until sundown, when the teacher himself was forced to go home to feed his chickens, milk his cow, or chop his kindling for his nighttime fire.

These teachers consistently broke most of the rules of modern psychology in their teaching methods. But they got results, even if our tender egos were no doubt bruised in the process. Numskullery was punished in the same fashion as mischief, disobedience, or inattention. Thumping of noggins, twisting of ears, cracking of pencils over poor dumb skulls were routine, with no stigma attached. Hand-slappings with a ruler, switchings for small fry, and whippings for older boys were administered for premeditated misconduct, with a certain knowledge on the pupil's part that when he got home the punishment would be repeated by his parents.

But for small infractions the memorizing of poetry, Bible verses, or of such noble passages as the Gettysburg Address, the Declaration of Independence, or "To be or not to be . . ." was the usual punishment. Before completing the twelfth grade I knew more declarations, poetry, and Scripture by heart than most modern youngsters ever read in so many years. But contrary to what might be expected, committing all these gems to memory did not make me hate poetry, good prose, or the Scripture. It did, however, prejudice me in favor of the old poets and the King James version of the Bible.

Strange as it may seem to youngsters of today, some of our privations afforded us some of our greatest pleasures. Would that overly permissive parents realized that the same might be true today. Our homemade desks, with lift-up lids to compartments designed for holding books, tablets, and pencils, were ample also for concealing all sorts of goodies and forbidden articles: licorice sticks and jawbreakers, chinquepins and goobers, marbles, jacks, and knives for playing mumbletypeg; frogs, lizards, June bugs, and buck-eye balls; tacks for putting in chair seats and rubber bands for slinging paper darts and spitballs; willow whistles and slingshots in the making—whatever treasure was in season or in vogue.

All unintentioned, these clumsy but indestructible objects were a boon to a child's well-being. His desk was a small sanctuary all his very own, a sort of nest for housing his prized objects, the acquiring of which fulfilled his pack-rat instincts. And in lifting the heavy lid he was momentarily hidden from the teacher—not for long, but for long enough to engage in any number of antics. The split-second protection of this bunker acted as a whetstone for a child's imagination and ingenuity in devising all sorts of schemes for tormenting his teacher and discomfiting his classmates. Behind these desk lids he may have become a fair soldier long before he was called on to don a uniform.

Far from being an irksome chore, the care and operation of the old castiron, potbellied stoves was a source of much coveted pleasure. Fires were built and stoked by boys, two by two, for a week at a time throughout the winter months. Never were stoves kept so infernally red-hot! The stokers found the fire in constant need of attention—the coal fetched in, ashes shaken down and taken out, clinkers removed, the water can on top replenished, the fire itself poked and punched into utmost performance throughout the day. Compared to staying still and studying, tending the fire was a picnic.

Obtaining water, drawn from a neighbor's well, was another coveted chore performed by boys, again selected to serve in pairs. Twice daily they were excused to fetch buckets of water, toted between them on a broom handle. As with the fire stokers, these drawers and fetchers of water discovered or invented a thousand emergencies demanding their attention along the way. Once the water was set on the shelf, we all drank from the same dipper. Consequently, we all had the same colds, the same mumps, measles, and chicken pox in as short a time as the germs could incubate. At least we were all comforted in our common afflictions.

The girls took turns sweeping the floor and washing the

blackboards and were compensated for jobs well done by gold stars on their report cards.

The rest rooms were two privies on opposite sides of the school ground, with high board fences about the front parts for privacy. Though icy cold in winter and not particularly pleasant in any weather, they were much in demand. But one had to raise a hand to get excused, and no two pupils were supposed to go at once. Usually the trip was unnecessary, but so greatly did some children fear disobeying the teacher, that the teacher's refusal occasionally led to disastrous results.

Shocking obscenities were scrawled on the walls of the girls' privy, and thus our innocent minds were early introduced to the forbidden world of sex—even before we understood the peculiar but undoubtedly wicked words. Knowing that these obscenities were put there by horrid boys, we girls despised their filthy, masculine minds, at the same time secretly envying them their worldly knowledge.

A small music room sat near the schoolhouse, where a music teacher labored mightily to instill into a few girls and boys enough musical ability to play "The Ripples of Alabama" and "Listen to the Mocking Bird," at which stage most pupils considered themselves sufficiently adept to need no further musical study. Although I never advanced to such difficult goals, I did fall under the spell of another's music, if melodious and not too minor-keyed. So much so, that to this good day whenever I hear simple scales rippling up and down the piano keyboard like a tinkling waterfall, I go into a sweet reverie as I did on crisp fall and balmy spring days when these same notes floated in pristine innocence from the open windows of the music room into the open windows of the schoolroom and put a spell on me.

No one would want to go back to these harsh old days, but in defending them, as old folks are apt to do, it can be said that what no one else had, no one missed; what no one else did, no one cared to do. Now in this day of excitement, glamor, extravagance, and social upheaval, one in which wants are manufactured and every desire demands instant gratification, sanity does beg us to borrow some simplicity from the past and apply it to our dangerous days in order to keep our earth sweet and clean and to damp down the fires of violent behavior. We must somehow minimize our wants and learn to be content with simpler ways and home-grown things.

Man is not so geared that he can constantly fight—himself, others, destiny—in order to get, to have, to be. We need to rediscover less demanding goals and be moved by gentler compulsions. Maybe in an awkward fashion this is what the "now" generation is trying to tell us.

If I have a serious complaint about my elders, it is that they built fires under us which set off many of the pressures and conflicts of the present day. Would that there had been no Horatio Alger books to read, fewer Edward Bok and Benjamin Franklin essays on how to succeed, less "Excelsior" poetry to learn and fewer high-minded and impractical axioms in our copybooks. "Hitch your wagon to a star" was the onward and upward cry of my generation. Well enough for a few but, sadly and surely, most of our wagons were fashioned to be hitched to mules, not to the breath-taking stars.

NINE

The Upside Down Case

In the thirties, as in previous times, custom in the Black Belt frowned on the employment of female teachers who were either homegrown or married. The thinking was that a hometown teacher would know too much about her pupils and their backgrounds not to show partiality, and they in turn would know the teacher too well to have the proper respect for her authority. In the second case, a married woman was considered a bad risk because of the danger of her becoming pregnant and of dividing her loyalties between home and school. There was the strong feeling that a married woman should stay at home, take care of her house, husband, and children, and not venture away from her God-given domestic duties.

Such custom may have worked considerable hardship on some women who would have liked to continue teaching after marriage, but it was a boon to single women who hoped their teaching certificates would be the magic to open the door of matrimony for them, a goal considerably more pressing to most of them than that of enlightening the youth of the land.

Thus each June saw thousands of teachers—some for better, some for worse—walking out of classroom doors into matrimonial traps, and each September saw thousands of others eagerly walking through these same doors, each with the hope in her heart that this time and this place would mark the lucky spot for snaring herself a husband. If perchance she did not find one within a year or two, she was smart to move on to another place, where she would be a new product in the old, old mating market.

This taboo against hiring hometown and married female teachers was as much a boon to unmarried men in a small community as it was to the teachers. Each fall these eligible males surveyed the new crop of teachers and staked out claims on those most appealing to their individual tastes. Some took the bait and got hooked for life; others were wary and kept on swimming around either for the fun of the game or because they weren't ready to relinquish their single cussedness.

But usually, in the end, these wary ones too, deciding that hot vittles and a warm bed were more to be desired than freedom, allowed themselves to be caught, sometimes to the consternation of old flames and acquaintances, by the quiet, home-body kind of girl whom they had previously ignored.

Except for the influx of new blood of these teachers and the exit of local females to other places, Camden might have become an inbred, odd-ball sort of place. But up one street and down another reside families whose mothers and grandmothers had once arrived as new teachers and who are still a leavening influence to the third and fourth generations.

Sadly, the time came, as it was bound to come, when school

authorities discovered that married women and home-town mothers probably made more dedicated and steadier teachers than the young unmarried girls who diverted so much of their time and energy into seeking mates. Hence teachers now (often unhappily) stay in their same old jobs until sickness or old age do finally part them.

For the former arrangement I can be truly thankful. For had it been otherwise, I might still be languishing in unmated limbo. But assurance that this would not be my fate did not come about soon enough to prevent me from thinking that I was headed for that state.

My classroom was in the old Female Institute building with its deeply worn stair treads, its cracked, creaking floors, and a huge silo-shaped stove for heating. But the windows were wide and airy. With them open, as we kept them in warm weather, one could feel the breezes, if any; and whether closed or open, one could see the leaves moving, the sky changing, people and vehicles passing, dogs frolicking on the grass and birds flying by—all giving us inside some contact with living and changing things of the world outside. (Pity the poor child housed in a steam-heated, airconditioned box with nothing but walls and a blackboard to look at, wrapped in wool, with no triggering mechanism for conjuring up daydreams or weaving fairy carpets on which to fly away to worlds of magic and make-believe.)

Older teachers, intending to be helpful, took me aside and informed me about matters which were well for me to know: who were members of the school board, who the local trustees—their children to be handled with a bit of extra care and attention—which mothers were thorns in the flesh and to be avoided if possible, which children could not learn and were merely carried along from grade to grade; which children were smarter (probably) than I was, which child's papers must be saved as proof or evidence of grades or cheating, and which people "ran" the school. Also, that it was an unwritten law that teachers attend the P.T.A. and all school functions, that it was wise to assign plenty of homework, and wiser to stay on top of my own.

One thing I was not told, and it startled me when I discovered it: some of my brightest pupils came from the most deprived families. Automatically I had assumed that the bright students, who always stand out like sunflowers in a cabbage patch, must come from the old, more affluent families of Camden. When I discovered that many of them came from little mule-and-wagon farms out in the back side of nowhere, I became a very humbled and sobered pupil myself. I still grieve over such youngsters—so much latent power hid under the bushel of hard necessity, when it should have eventually commanded the genii of test tubes, wielded the doctor's scalpel, or opened and sharpened minds of lesser light.

Most of the youngsters were robust and rambunctious, but there were a few pasty faces, big-eyed and apathetic, apparently victims of pure laziness. At first they got little sympathy, but after weeks of effort on my part without response, I appealed to the principal. He suggested they be sent to the health department for examination. It was discovered that they were victims of roundworm or hookworm, which once eliminated, allowed these children to open up like crocuses after a long winter's sleep.

There were sporadic epidemics of the communicable diseases, and then a prolonged and stubborn infestation of head lice—probably spreading from the cloakroom, where some afflicted child had hung a coat and the vermin had crawled to other coats and at last onto the heads of the other children. There was a great outcry from the mamas, but nothing less than treating heads with lard and kerosene and burning sulphur candles in the cloakroom finally exterminated the pests.

Later in the winter came the sneezing, sniffling, and coughing. Those who developed fever and had to be kept home were said to have grippe or flu—a bug that, since the plague of World War I, had been treated with the utmost respect. When chattering chills and searing fever became rampant, recurring in greater severity every seventh day, we knew that malaria was on the march, and it was time for quinine and spring tonic. Another ailment, which afflicted a few and was dreaded by all, was the seven-year itch. In previous years it was practically incurable—hence its name. By the year 1933 there was a remedy, but it was greasy and messy and required persistent application for weeks. Consequently, its eradication was rarely accomplished by school's close.

According to precedents of what sort of discipline was proper, my own left much to be desired. I felt constantly frustrated, knowing that I might have taught more to those willing to learn had I been able to make the few who were dedicated to mischief-making behave. There was the boy who could shatter the peace by crossing his eyes like Ben Turpin, another who got the attention I begged for by wiggling his ears, and another who could crack his knuckles like a pop-gun and defy detection even while I looked him straight in the face. Other distractions went on interminably.

Unfortunately, I was of an age and temperament that led me to believe that any child could be appealed to and won over by love, reason, and patience. If I was right about some, I was dead wrong with others; and these were my hair shirt the whole year through. However, could they have known it, my sympathies were often with them, for I knew that to be quiet and still was as unnatural for a boy as for a puppy. Besides, I had lived long enough to know that restless, innovative youngsters would usually do better in later life than the quiet docile ones. Actually, I more often wanted to laugh with them than to scold them. I rather believe they sensed as much and consequently gave me a harder time than they otherwise might have.

The hot dusty days of September finally passed. Then one night in late October the sky glowered; lightning split it with sulfurous thunderclaps and opened the flumes of heaven. Rain drenched the thirsty earth, purging it sweet-clean and dew-cool. Nights and days shook off their oppressive heat. Fall had arrived.

Then it was that hill and dale went wild with breath-taking color: the blood-red gums, the burnished gold hickories, the shaded pink- and green-gold maples, the great garnet oaks, the orange, red, and even purple-hued sassafras, the claret sumac lit by its burgundy candles, the now crimson dogwood with its red berries; the straws, the tans, and browns of other trees mingled with the everlasting green of the pines—all blended into a mosaic of loveliness which made the heart ache and rejoice together.

The aroma of frying bacon and wood smoke was my morning tonic; the odors of fresh milk, of quick-kindling fires and biscuits baking, my twilight balm. The immediate past, which had encased me, began to crack and peel, and my spirit to sing again as it had not done since I was very young and had lived in a world of wondrous sights and sounds, feelings and imaginings, unpolluted by trouble or the ails or ills of mankind.

As I walked to school in the early morning I saw again—as I had not seen since I dawdled to school barefoot an aeon ago—the spider-web wheels whose strands shimmered like fairy necklaces with droplets of midnight mists; during quiet times at evening I saw again—as I had not seen since I was an adolescent and foolishly sentimental—the iridescent sunsets, which spread themselves like chameleon banners across the sky. Odors of souring scuppernongs, of rotting pears, of cotton, of fodder, of molding leaves, all nurtured the seed sown in some hidden recess of my consciousness and woke them to joy—the simple joy of seeing and feeling and being alive.

The cotton wagons groaning to market, the clipclopping of hooves, the hum of a gin, the whine of saws, the lowing of cattle, came alive again and became a part of the throbbing of my heart, keeping time to some rhythm, some design, some meaning for things far beyond my power to discern. Life, ebbing and flowing, receding and rebounding, flowing for me as some distant incoming tide—without shape or substance as yet—but with myself, at last, a part of the rhythm, no longer a derelict bit of flotsam.

My life was simple. It had to be. But I had a roof over my

head. I was earning a living and paying my way. I was busy by day. At night I was tired. I slept with peace, I rose with hope, and dined with faith. Not bad company these three. But there was one thing lacking—especially when one felt the rhythm of the universe pulsing in one's veins.

TEN

A Wall There Was

Soon after the Civil War a singular thing occurred in Camden and Wilcox County, a thing that added a red-pepper zing to the still-raw wounds of the natives. A band of Scotch Presbyterians, most of them only once removed from the old country and Yankees to the core, migrated from the North to settle here, not as speculators but as people seeking permanent homes. William Henderson, the first to arrive, had been a captain in the Union army, and having been stationed for a time in central Alabama and liking the land and climate, he decided to leave the winter snows and boggy springs of his Ohio settlement and make his home in a place less hostile to his chosen livelihood of farming. After he had settled near Camden, others of his kin and friends, all of like faith, soon followed. One kinsman, John Russell Liddell, settled in Camden.

David Liddell, father of the John Russell Liddell who came south, had come to America in about 1839 to spy out the land. He returned to Scotland and came back in 1840 as one of a group of sixty seeking homes in the New World, some of whom, himself included, settled in and around Wooster, Ohio.

These Scotsmen were a staunch breed, and they had to be to survive. Even their storm-tossed passage of six weeks in a sailing ship—during which water had to be rationed to half a cup a day per person—was proof of their vigor. The photographs of most of these men show them to have been as stern as the Great Stone Face, eagle-eyed, with strong features, corrugated faces, chins and jowls obscured by a bib of grizzled whiskers. There was one exception. The picture of David Liddell shows him to have had sparkling eyes and a broad smile, as if the picture taking had been a big joke. I am thankful for that picture. It explains why his grandson, Will Liddell, could never be the stern, dour person usually portrayed as the prototype of his forebears.

Though David Liddell was strict so far as his religious convictions were concerned, he lived by the golden rule. He was a friend of the poor and outcast, even fitting up a room over his workshop to accommodate tramps, beggars, and men hunting work. An Irishman sought lodging there one Saturday night. When he rose on the following morning he announced that he must be going. "Na, na," said David, "you'll na be breaking the Sabbath by traveling aboot on the Lord's day." Thus rebuked, the Irishman sat down. Pretty soon he remarked, "That's a good stove you have there. How much did it cost you?" "There now," said David Liddell, "we'll na be talking about the price of a stove on the Sabbath day." What they did talk about is not known, but my guess is that the Irishman accompanied his host to church and heard a sermon to keep him straight for whatever journey lay ahead.

These Scots' coming here at such a time is difficult to understand. It was as if sane and sensible people were knowingly and willingly casting themselves into still-blazing remnants of a mighty bonfire. Naturally, the defeated, dispossessed, and despairing Rebels greeted their erstwhile Yankee enemies as they might have greeted the plagues of Pharaoh. Already hounded by conniving carpetbaggers, the natives lumped these immigrants into the same despised category and treated them similarly.

The usual warm Southern hospitality was frozen into a special brand of Southern hostility reserved only for the conquering enemy, and its venom was deadly indeed. When these strangers arrived, no one welcomed them with friendly greeting or neighborly calls. No one took them peace offerings of pats of butter or flower cuttings. No one offered to sit with their babies or help nurse their sick. Southern ladies lifted their skirts in disdain when passing them, even in the church pews; some of the men were threatened with violence, one at least was shot at, with the bullet going through his clothing instead of his heart. Their children were unwelcome in such schools as there were, so their elders set up a school of their own and hired a teacher to instruct them or took them back up North to schools more friendly.

These undaunted people, in spite of the wall built to isolate them, bought land, went into businesses, worked like Trojans and lived like Spartans, paid their debts, went to church, besought the Almighty's aid, kept their mouths shut, and found comfort and consolation in their common problems and simple, common joys. But the wall stood.

Eventually, through the charity of the church, the first stones fell. Though taken in reluctantly by the Southern Presbyterian Church—parted during the war years from the Northern Church—these Scotch Presbyterians were no fair-weather Christians. They worked at their faith, consequently took hold of the handle offered them and busied themselves in the Lord's vineyard as best they could. They superintended and taught Sunday School and Bible classes, they sponsored choir practice and prayer meetings, paid their preacher generously and entertained visiting preachers and missionaries gladly. They opened the church doors, built the fires, brought the altar flowers, and were eternally and unfailingly present, rain or shine, heat or cold. No doubt the native church members began to be greatly relieved to have such ready help in keeping the wheels of the church greased; hence, before many years, they rewarded their former enemies—who out-Calvinized themselves—with a certain amount of genuine trust, accord, and good will.

Probably the next breach in the wall came from among the young. Though the new generation born here to these people were still called Yankees and would be for many years, they were less and less called damn-Yankees; and gradually, the school yielding its grudge, the children mingled freely with others their own age, even though they had to defend their rights with fist-fights or by allying themselves with bigger and stronger boys for protection.

Another section of the wall, which soon went down, was in the area of business, farming and merchandizing in particular. Captain Henderson, who became Judge Henderson during Reconstruction—and a good judge he was—bought land wherever he could find it to buy, much of it considered worn out and unfit for farming, and began some new-fangled methods of farming that boggled the imaginations of the local farmers.

These farmers had judged "he had bit off more'n he could chew," and that "he'd have to sleep in a horse trough 'fore he paid out the land," but they were later forced to eat their words. When Judge Henderson began to rotate his crops, diversify his farming operations, inaugurate conservation methods, and actually put fertilizer on the land, old slave farmers predicted that "it'd never 'mount to nothing." But when an acre of land began to produce two and three times as much cotton as it had produced previously, when the judge had cows and other livestock to sell from land that had been abandoned for cropping and lately produced nothing but sedge grass and rabbits, people came from all around to inquire about and to see these unheard-of results. The judge's adage of "Plant a paying crop and leave the land better," had replaced the old order of "Farm the land until worn out and then move on."

Similarly, by careful buying, close but courteous selling, store-keeping from sunup to bedtime and bookkeeping half the night and on holidays, merchandizing paid off and won respect in its way. People began to depend on these Scotch storekeepers for honesty and respect them for their hard work and fair figuring.

Another door was opened in the wall by the womenfolk. They worked from both sides and met in the middle. The southern gentlewomen who were finding life difficult as well as barren in these postwar days began to appreciate the accomplishments of these Yankee women, and the Yankee women were equally happy to find a response to their accomplishments and acceptance by the Southern women. They soon found rapport through their mutual efforts in music, art, writing, teaching, and handiwork. And they followed it up with much visiting and working together in Missions, in W.C.T.U., and in playing flinch and charades, and putting on concerts, Chatauquas, minstrels, and ice-cream suppers.

Though the political portion of the wall was more difficult to breach, it was inevitable from the start that eventually this would crumble also. At first, naturally, the Republican Party of these Abolitionist Scots was beyond the pale to Southern Democrats, now made uncompromisingly bitter by the war and its aftermath. These Jacksonian Democrats now became known as Yellow-Dog Democrats—that is, they would vote for a yellow dog before voting Republican. But time brought its termites. Some had already been at work in the Democratic edifice when Franklin Roosevelt let loose a swarm of them that so infuriated the faithful that they began to desert their party in droves. But because they could not as yet accept shelter under the Republican roof, they began to spin off into tangents like the Dixiecrats, a group that they felt better reflected their feelings.

At the same time that these red-blooded Southerners were infuriated by doles, hand-outs, and federal interference with local government, the hard-working, careful-spending Republicans were equally incensed. Here, at long last, they were able to join hands and hearts with the Southern landowners and the "old rebel" families who had become Dixiecrats, Independents, or quiet and uncommitted Republicans. The dyed-in-the-hide conservatives of both groups, starting from opposite poles, had finally found a common meeting ground in their political thinking. Thus another arch in the wall collapsed.

But perhaps the span that most bitterly and vehemently divided the groups at first was that of racial matters, mixed or unmixed with politics. And the strangest thing of all is the way these Yankees personally dynamited this span in the wall and came over, comfortably reconciling themselves with the most stubborn and die-hard segregationists. But this, like their politics, was not so strange as it might seem. These Scotsmen deplored what they perceived as the Negro's light-hearted attitude toward life—the lassitude, the lack of initiative, the improvidence—whatever their ultimate causes.

(Seeing the Negro's need of help and enlightenment, Judge Henderson was instrumental in getting the Northern Presbyterian Church to promote the building and operation of four mission schools in Wilcox County, which taught not only the three Rs, but sewing, cooking, nursing, and manual skills. In addition the judge taught the Bible to his farm hands each Sunday afternoon, and in the field he taught them better methods of farming than they had learned as slaves.)

Furthermore, these Yankees strongly believed that intermingling of the races would lead to miscegenation and eventually to that estate contemptuously referred to as "mongrelization." This is what most white Southerners believed, hence both felt that segregation of the races was not only right but necessary. It was not strange, then, that these Yankees and the Black Belt Southerners should fight side by side in the long battle against integration.

It was not easy for the Yankee men to enter into the social life of the southern menfolk. About everything the male Southerner did for fun, these Scotsmen felt was either sinful or foolish. They had no time for hunting or fishing or frolicking around; they had no money to throw away on drinking, gambling, or horseracing, not even on smoking or high living. Consequently, they had, at first, small meeting ground with Southern men in their social life. But time mended this gap. As the older Scots became more affluent, their sons cracked the thrifty family mold and now their grandchildren have completely broken free of the old puritanical inhibitions against spending money for pleasure, playing around, and having more fun in life. Now they "do their own things," which happen to be the same things their Old-South family friends do and enjoy. Now that children and grandchildren of both groups freely intermarry, the two old enemy factions have literally, as well as figuratively, gone to bed together. As one Yankee descendant remarked, "Our granddaddies gave 'em hell down here once upon a time; now we come along and marry these southern girls, and they're giving it right back to us."

The old spite wall has, indeed, crumbled. First here, then there, now everywhere. It is both interesting and amusing to see what wounds time can heal. Frost knew what he was talking about when he wrote—"Something there is that does not love a wall."

ELEVEN
_____

There Is a Tide

School went along as schools must do, and the days stretched out and the nights went by without any change in my social status. But the sands of fate were shifting. Fortunately, I had elected to go to the Presbyterian Church, the church of Will Liddell, previously mentioned, grandson of the Scotch immigrant, David Liddell. Importantly for me, Will Liddell was one of the persons on whom my sister had put her stamp of approval, and incidentally he sang in the choir. Thus, when I was asked to join that group, it seemed the part of wisdom to accept.

Although I could sing about as well as a cow could dance, great talent was evidently not a requisite for this honor. I noticed that Will Liddell himself sang much as though calling cows, and though there *were* a few accomplished singers in the group, most of them were no better qualified than I. At least I could hold a book, open and shut my mouth, and only pretend to sing when the going got rough.

Perhaps this is what others of them should have done, for the remark was made about certain members who were trying too valiantly, with tremolos and falsettos, that they should either take voice or take poison. A future sister-in-law recalled that as a bride she had felt it her bounden duty to sing in this choir and did so until her parents visited her. After services that Sabbath morning, her father took her aside and remarked, in regard to her singing, "In heaven's name, Laura, do you *have* to do that?" It was the end of her vocal career. Fortunately or unfortunately, however one looks at it, I had no one to so admonish me.

However greatly the congregation may have suffered from my efforts, they paid off in my behalf, for around Thanksgiving—and it was a time for thanksgiving on my part—Will Liddell asked if he might escort me to choir practice. He might and he did. And that was the beginning—the hinge of fate, as it were, which opened the door to my future life in Camden.

But it was entirely too early to be sure of anything. I could only hope that heaven would be kind and luck on my side. Yet, from this time on there were not enough hours in the day to do justice to all my interests. Inside the classroom I did what I reasonably could to uphold the teaching profession; outside I did all in my power to assure my removal from it.

In spite of being just half Yankee, as most people would concede since he was born here, Will was a man made to warm a woman's heart. His ears stood out like sails—a sure sign of honesty and candor—and from his mouth and eyes crinkled happiness lines like those of his grandfather's. He was all extrovert, activist, completely conformed to his family, church, and his Deep South environment—never questioning, doubting, criticizing, or complaining. His oldest brother, Roy, continued the mercantile business established by his father; he and the other brothers, John and Glen, operated the electric power plant that served Camden and outlying areas, ginned cotton, made and delivered ice, ground meal, mixed feed and fertilizer. The family definitely did not believe in carrying all its eggs in one basket.

Like almost every other businessman, Will operated a small

farm as a sort of hobby, but the power business required most of his time and energy. Since he was the outside man of the firm, he called himself the "pole-cat." He recalls with some pride that he hung the first transformer ever hung in Wilcox County. For many years the poles were cedars cut from the woods, limbed and brought in on lumber trucks, manually installed by "huff and heft." One of his "grunters," as the ground helpers were called, remarked that Mister Will's "sperit" was sometimes too fast, but that he never asked anybody to do anything he wouldn't tackle himself. His favorite expression was, "If you can lift your end, I can lift mine."

He often laughed about some of his experiences. On one occasion he was planning to cut in the home of an elderly gentlewoman whose past glory may have faded but whose pride was by no means diminished. Observing the work crew preparing to come into her place from the front, which was the shortest and customary way of entering, she came out and demanded that the line be brought in to her house from the rear. "Electricity," she remonstrated, "is a servant, and servants enter my house from the rear." Although more work and poles were required to do the job, her wishes were deferred to.

Another time he needed to "guy" a pole that stood on the premises of a new customer—in this case a stranger. A slab of concrete, onto which the guy-wire must be fastened, was called by the construction crew a "dead man" and was buried a few feet from the base of the pole. Not wishing to dig on a person's property without asking permission, Will went to the man's house and called to see him. Never dreaming that he might be misunderstood, Will matter-of-factly asked if he might bury a dead man on his front lawn. The man staggered back as if hit by a sledge hammer. "My God, man!" he gulped. "Have you killed somebody?"

In those days ice was delivered by ice-wagon, drawn by old Mamie, an educated mule if there ever was one. She made her rounds so often that she knew the route and her routine by heart, stopping where she was supposed to stop and starting when she heard the ice-hooks dropped into the wagon. "Coote" Dexter was the iceman, and though old Mamie was a jewel, Coote had his problems with her. When a customer would move or trade in his wooden icebox for an electric refrigerator, old Mamie would persist in stopping as usual and refuse to leave until Coote got out, went around to the back of the wagon, and after a few moments, noisily dropped his hooks into the wagon as if completing a delivery. Only then would Mamie resume her duties. For a new customer, Coote carried a heavy iron weight for hitching Mamie until she learned to stop there also.

Besides Mamie, Coote had problems with his customers. Some who had huge, dilapidated boxes would buy only a dime's worth of ice daily and then fume and complain about its being porous or milky or just not cold, because it melted so rapidly. Others complained of short weights for the same reason; widows wanted cats helped down out of trees, drunks wanted Coote to fetch them more liquor, and small fry followed the wagon to get ice shavings or just a chunk of ice to suck through a rag or handkerchief. But Coote never argued with anyone and never refused a favor even if it took all day instead of a half day to make his rounds.

But the time came, as the old iceboxes wore out and were thrown on the garbage dump or relegated to attics and barns, that electric refrigerators came into their own, and then it was that old Mamie lost her job and Coote was transferred to another. Years have passed, and now, in this fantastic day of flying to the moon, young people are resurrecting these old relics, remodeling them, and calling them antiques. Thus it is that yesterday's rubbish becomes tomorrow's treasure.

But to return to Will Liddell. Quite naturally, he did not drink. Drinking was an expensive habit for a Scotsman; and had it been free, it would have been outlawed in his family with as much horror as the use of hard drugs is frowned on in a respectable family today. For their abstinence, Will and his brothers were often considered daft. On one occasion, preparing to go deep-sea fishing off the Gulf Coast, they hired a boat, with skipper, to take them out. The skipper watched with interest as they hauled in their food and fishing gear. Finally, when they were apparently finished, he wanted to know if they had forgotten their liquor. "There won't be any liquor," they assured him. "Well," said the skipper, "what the hell you going fishing for?"

When visiting within my own big family, where it had been customary for father to take his toddy on Sunday mornings and icy days and where my brothers could take it or leave it—sometimes when young they didn't leave it soon enough—I told them about Will and how, during intermissions in our very rare dances, instead of producing a hip-flask, he would take me to the ice-house where the family's fresh milk was refrigerated in huge coolers, and would pour us mugs of ice-cold milk for refreshment. At this my brothers whooped in amusement and amazement and wondered what kind of curious creature I had discovered. They warned me that a man who was forty years old and had never tasted liquor was too good to be true, and that I would do well to watch my step.

TWELVE

Getting Acquainted

Afternoon fires sent lazy smoke from house chimneys, frosty mornings brought jackets out of mothballs, and finally a crackling freeze stripped the bright leaves from the trees and withered the fall flowers. Winter, though never feeling sure of itself in Alabama, had arrived. It was a strenuous time for me, the days too short and the nights not long enough to include a whole new field of interest in my schedule.

Feeling it to be the pleasantest pastime available, Will took me, when time and weather permitted, on small hunting expeditions after school and on Saturdays. I could never get set, aim, and fire at the jet-propelled quail until it was a mile away, and the first time I tried, the automatic knocked me ignominiously backward, as flat as a butter paddle. Hence I confined my shooting to a 410 shotgun and a .22 rifle. With them I could sometimes hit a hawk sitting on a fence post, a rabbit about to run, or a squirrel attempting to camouflage himself by immobility. I was no huntswoman. But I persevered.

We sometimes carried the makings of a picnic, barbecuing a young squirrel, Indian fashion, for our *pièce de résistance.* I must admit there was plenty of resistance on the part of the squirrel thus prepared, but I swore otherwise and would have eaten it had I been forced to swallow it whole.

My grocery bill was considerably lightened during these days with the game and turnips and sweet potatoes that Will brought in. There being no place to eat out, the idea was mine to invite him to sometimes eat in with me. How I survived the cooking of birds and biscuits and turnip greens on a balky, smoky kerosene stove I'll never know, nor how our digestions handled the results. But survive we did.

With my small son in tow, Will took us chinquepin and chestnut hunting. He knew, too, where the muscadines and persimmons grew. We peeled and chewed sugar cane, ate rock-hard pears, and picked goobers from freshly pulled-up vines. Such treasured goodies were handy booty for acquiring a rabbit foot, buckeye balls, or agates at school, but eaten surreptitiously and in quantity they provoked some exquisite stomach aches and terrifying nightmares.

On several bright harvest nights we went to the plantation to watch the Negroes making their yearly supply of syrup, some from sorghum, some from blue-ribbon sugar cane. The juice was already boiling in the shallow pans mounted over cemented rock ovens, in which booming fires, fed by heart pine (called light'ood) blazed brightly and belched streaks of flame and tar-black smoke from their flues like fire-breathing dragons of old.

The old mule would be walking dejectedly (dejectedly, no doubt, because he never arrived at a destination), round and round on his circular path, pulling the grinders, while someone fed in the cane, the juice going through a strainer into a barrel and the "chaws" deposited on the other side. Periodically new juice was poured into the upper ends of the pans as the syrup was drawn off, fully cooked, from the lower ends. Cooking took place as the juice slowly made its way around panel barriers from the higher to the lower level of the pans.

Women stood by the pans, skimming the scummy flotsam from the syrup with shovellike paddles; yellow jackets swarmed over the sweet-sour skimmings, apparently drunk or gorged enough to pay no attention to their human enemies. Both workers and lookers-on had a sort of end-of-harvest frolic, the older ones joshing each other and telling tall tales, then kidding the younger ones, who hung their heads, looking sheepish, but laughed along, saying little or nothing to defend themselves.

The yeasty, sweetish vapor from the big pans was tantalizingly fragrant, and the odor of the freshly drawn syrup so robust and mouth-watering that one wished for a hot biscuit for sopping the pan.

Here I came to meet, some for the first time, many of the Negroes living in this river bend, called Oliver's, most of whom I knew for a long while only by nickname or first name. There were Fox, Scat, Rat, Cat, Monkey, Possum; Pa Man, Babe Bunk, Ike; Uncle Joe and Aunt Mary, Carney and Aunt Lou, John Henry and Baby, Van and Mammy, Sam and Ada, Hot Shot and Pickaninny, Sunk and Ella, many of them Pettways or Aikens. The homes of those living on Will's place clustered on a spot of high ground called "the quarters." These tenants I came to know more intimately and to love, as time went on.

Carney was then the head cow-man. He was the one who, when Will's riding horse died from snake-bite, temporarily forcing Will to ride the pasture on a mule, took his boss man to task for this undignified mode of transportation and consequent loss of face among other tenants of nearby plantations. "Mister Will," he scolded Will kindly, "I don't want my boss riding a mule like me. It ain't seemly. You got to get a hoss, or else I'll have to get down and walk."

Although such status symbols are largely resented nowadays, the cow-boss who replaced Carney, Willie Aiken, known as Sunk, had much the same attitude. He, too, felt a reflected pride in his white folks and their possessions, how they looked and how they acted. Sunk called the cows "us cows" and attended to them as if they were his own, and if Mister Will didn't keep his herd free of scrawnies and uglies, Sunk would readily complain. "I don't want folks making fun of us cows," he'd say. And often he chided Will about his dilapidated truck and his beat-up hats and jackets. "They ain't fittin' fer you," he'd protest.

Sunk was proud of his faithful, hard-working wife Ella, as well he should have been. "I got a good wife," he once boasted to Will. "We been married forty years, and I ain't had to slap her down yet."

As fate would have it, Sunk, who never shot craps or drank liquor or fooled around with women, was just once in his life persuaded to mind a run of "shinny" for a friend and got caught at the still. While he spent months paying off a fine for making the stuff, the real culprit went scot-free, moved into another bend of the river, and continued his moonshine operations.

There was Van, a tenant farmer, and his wife Mammy. Van, tall and lean, was bent like a bow from leaning his back to the plow, to the cotton boll, from bearing burdens too heavy, ever since he was big enough to lift a hoe—the heaviest being his burden of nine head o' chillun. Mammy, ample and able, her front teeth prominently gold-capped, was pleasant and affable, but she could be otherwise. She claimed that she could back-slap a young-un out the back door with one hand and never stop what she was doing with the other.

Poor Van. One day he came creeping into town; and since landlords customarily stood for their tenants' doctor bills, he asked Will to please send him to the doctor. Will wanted to know what in the world ailed him, head tied up, eyes swollen, back hunkered over.

"Mammy and me had a little fuss," Van admitted.

"What you been up to, Van?" Will asked, knowing what

caused most family fusses. "Mister Will, I ain't done nothing," he insisted. "But somebody told a wrong on me, and Mammy believed 'em."

"Looks like you got the worst of the racket," Will suggested.

"Sho' did, Mister Will. Mammy caught me while I was sleep and hit me with a shoe las'."

"Shoe last? Great guns, man, she might have killed you. Why in blazes didn't you take the thing away from her?"

"To tell the truth, Mister Will, after the first lick, I warn't able."

Van was still young and vigorous when he went off visiting to Mobile. While there, he later claimed, a man with an evil eye hoo-dooed him. He knew when it happened. This man had jabbed him with the end of an umbrella, and being startled, Van had dropped his hat. The stranger picked it up and after inspecting it had handed it back. When Van got home he found a strange yellow powder inside the hatband. Van knew that he'd been conjured. He lost his appetite. He couldn't sleep. He couldn't work. He turned ashy gray and his eyes sank back into his skull. The medical doctor could do him no good. Van wasted away and died—a victim of his own fear.

And who could forget Uncle Joe Garrett, only once removed from slavery, and his wife, Aunt Mary, with their family of ten? Uncle Joe's arms hung loose and curved inward toward his knees, which bent low as he walked. Uncle Joe admitted that he had "laid up" with his first wife for five years, but because she hadn't brought him any children, he had sent her home and taken Mary. But, now that he and Mary had their house bulging with children, he left the toting, fetching, hoeing, and cotton-picking to them while he spent his days and many of his nights in the woods and on the river fishing, hunting, and trapping. His clothing was so patched by Aunt Mary that no detective could have discovered which parts were of the original garments; and his shoes, scraps of leather tied together with string, flapped and fluttered as he moved along like a walking scarecrow.

Late in life Uncle Joe was persuaded that he must be baptized in order to be saved. The baptizing was done in a nearby creek and because of his age Uncle Joe was the first and most important candidate for salvation that day. The preacher didn't realize it, but when he dunked Uncle Joe, his head lodged under a tree root growing into the water's edge. Probably aroused by the commotion from his hole in the bank, a moccasin at this particular moment came swimming toward the preacher, who immediately forgot his business and started clambering up the bank as fast as he could. Uncle Joe, meanwhile supposing that the preacher was still holding him under water, remained calm for a moment until finally, about to suffocate, he began to thrash around in an effort to free himself. When at last he came up sputtering to the surface, all but dead for air, he looked up and saw the preacher safe and sound on the bank. As soon as he got breath enough to speak, he remarked in all charity, "Damn it, Preacher, if you gotta drown me to get me to heaven, then I'll jes' go to hell."

There was Felix Pettway, known as Scat. Scat was the best 'coon hunter in Oliver's Bend. He kept a pack of 'coon hounds and with them he rarely came home without the limit. By selling 'coon meat which was, and still is, in great demand, for three dollars a 'coon, and 'coon pelts, Scat was able to feed his hounds and pay for his ammunition. He claimed there were thirty-two musk glands in the animal, which had to be carefully removed before cooking. "If one was left," he said, "you could smell him a mile." After the dressed 'coon was boiled in hot pepper and salt water, it was baked in the oven with a barbecue sauce. The meat was gamey but good—that is, if one's taste were not too finicky or prejudiced against 'coon meat.

As a young man, while logging, Scat received a serious back injury, caused by a log breaking from its loading chain, wheeling about, and slamming him across the back. For three years he suffered periodic torture and partial paralysis until the local doctor finally gave up treating him and sent him off to see a bone surgeon. This specialist, after examining the X-rays and finding a very complicated condition, hesitated to operate. Only as a last resort did he finally do so. After the operation,

Scat was taken to a ward where the doctor told the nurse in charge to "just keep him as comfortable as possible. He'll be dead in three days."

Subsequently the doctor dismissed Scat from his mind. A week later when he happened to be back in the ward he all but had apoplexy himself when he saw Scat sitting up in bed flexing his legs. From that moment Scat's case became the doctor's special project. Scat stood, he walked, he was dismissed. When he went back a few weeks later for a check-up, the nurse got out his file, looked at Scat, shook her head, and asked for some identification. Scat presented his driver's license. The nurse was still dubious. "I hope you're on the level," she said, "because you're supposed to be dead. Your file is stamped 'deceased'."

Scat was far from dead. He did continue to have considerable pain, however, which the doctor said he would have to live with. In time, Scat heard about the curative power of goat's milk, so he bought a pair of milk goats of a very fine breed and began drinking their milk. He swears this cured him. Something did. To see him catch a yearling from horseback and then bull-dog him to the ground into abject submission, one would never believe he had come so near being a wheel-chair case. He has had other brushes wih violent death, but he dismissed them lightly, with complete faith that it wasn't his time to go.

There were others, good friends, good people. Maybe they were not too unhappy then, for they did not know how deprived they were, living in their shuttered cabins plastered with magazine paper to keep out the wind and cold, going to the spring for water; boiling, heating, and cooking with hand-chopped wood, and having so few comforts and conveniences. But, too, they were spared the blare and rush of today, the strain and drain of paying for houses and cars and the dissatisfaction of not being able to gratify every whim and fancy.

The good old days were not good for the Negro. The fine new days are still not the best for him, but he is on his way—in a hurry. But before we look ahead, perhaps it would be well to take a backward look at our Negro friends in the Black Belt.

THIRTEEN

The Black Burden

Mark Twain once said in his autobiography that about certain matters he held two opinions, one private and one public. About race and religion most people in the Black Belt hold similar opinions, and wisely so, for if one made all of his opinions on these subjects public, he would probably be lynched before sundown.

From viewing the placid demeanor of members of any church congregation, one might assume that all wholly agreed with the doctrine and theology expounded from the pulpit. Yet if one were able to peer inside each skull and read the thinking there, he no doubt would find that many differ somewhat, and some drastically. But because most churchgoers have good manners and a modicum of plain horse sense, those who do differ keep their shirts on and their mouths shut.

Consequently, I am aware that I may have to pay for discussing racial matters, but to avoid the subject in writing about a place where in 1933 there were four blacks to one white (and in this present time two to one) would be like omitting the nervous system when trying to explain how the body functions.

To begin at the beginning, one must go back—one must always go back when trying to understand the South, particularly in regard to racial matters. Hence to understand the racial conflict in the 1960s, one must go back, not necessarily to the Civil War, which was prologue to what followed, but to Reconstruction days. What happened then might be considered the beginning of our great racial drama. But the drama was not allowed to play itself out in those long-ago days because the curtain was rung down after the first act for an intermission that lasted for nearly a hundred years.

But neither play nor players were dead. The curtain went up again in the 1950s and 1960s; and, as if time had stood still, Act Two was begun, and the play went on until Act Three climaxed with solutions that were shattering to most southern whites.

But why, one might ask, did it require such a violent eruption to break the mold that seemed to have encased Southern whites for so long? If it was the result of Reconstruction, as many believe, why was the emotional impact so powerful as to blind so many to inevitable changes? For the sake of charity and clarity, this era seems to warrant a bare-boned review.

My father's generation was deep-dyed with remembrances of this unfortunate time. They had suffered through its aftermath, they had suffered from it, and if their efforts to build back their broken lives were not the best, they excused their actions as being not a fault of themselves but of a necessity born of Reconstruction. But because the men of my family were moderate and fair-minded in their attitude toward race relations, I early realized that the tragedy of this unhappy time was not a single but a two-pronged one, tragic for the Negro as well as for the white. Consequently, when Acts Two and Three of this racial drama were played out in recent years, it was a tug-of-war for one who could see what happened to both sides in the past and who could sympathize with both antagonist and protagonist in the present. It was not an easy spot to be in, but that is where I stood.

But to return to Act One: the Civil War was over; the South was prostrate, penniless; Lincoln, with his good will and plans for reconciliation toward the South, was dead. Radicals who wished to punish the South had taken the reins of power in Washington, and punish they did; freeing the slaves without compensation to their owners, denying the Southern states reentry into the Union until constitutions acceptable to Congress were drafted and the Fourteenth Amendment had been ratified disenfranchising white males who had been active in support of the Confederacy while enfranchising male freed-men, dividing the South into military districts administered by Federal generals, and allowing rascals and despoilers to exploit the vanquished and helpless states. As James Truslow Adams says, "The war left the South prostrate, Reconstruction left it maddened."

And how did our four million slaves fare? Freed with extravagant promises, yet not receiving even the forty acres and a mule, stripped of the only security they had ever known, they were set free to wander homeless, jobless, penniless, over the land, to scrounge for a living. The result was that the white man's fear of what these rootless vagabonds might do set into motion all sorts of rumors, the most inflammatory being that of the danger of rape. Though rarely proven to be true, this rumor spread like a prairie fire to panic proportions, further hindering the efforts of these nomads to find a safe haven or even shelter for their heads. Those who remained with their old masters probably did so as much out of necessity as from loyalty, but many did stay.

And, alas, it was true and not just rumor, that unscrupulous northern adventurers were using these freedmen as pawns, promoting wild schemes for the adventurer's own benefit, which cost the already bankrupt South millions of dollars borrowed at exorbitant interest from northern banks. They put former slaves into political power and prominence where, naturally, they made a mockery of the legislative process and offended whites with behavior that was to be expected of uneducated slaves suddenly thrust into places of power and prestige. All these things caused the only people who understood them or could really help them, to fear, distrust, and despair of them.

Added to these ills, the traumatic experience by white men of being subjected to domination by their former slaves, who greatly outnumbered them, bore directly and mightily on the Southern white man's fear of the power of the Negro, whether political, economic, or social. Thus the bitterest and most long-lasting fruit of Reconstruction, a direct result of this fear, was the determination of the white man to put the Negro back into his "place" of powerlessness, and at all costs to keep him there.

And there was also at that time a belief—belief because it had never been given a chance to be proven otherwise—that the Negro race was an inferior one. This belief added weight to the fear that if the Negro remained in power, integration would follow, intermarriage would result, and the purity of the white race would ultimately be destroyed. Although much interbreeding had already been accomplished, the argument against it helped to promote and keep alive the determination of whites to maintain the separation of races in all their affairs.

There was no doubt in the minds of the vanquished rebels as to where the power lay. It was in the ballot box. And as soon as Federal troops were withdrawn from the South and moderation returned to Washington, they concentrated on winning back that power. They did it by fair means and foul. They stuffed the ballot boxes, they destroyed them after counting the votes of both the quick and the dead. And where blacks outnumbered whites, as they did in the Black Belt, another method was put into practice—intimidation of the blacks. Thus was born the Ku Klux Klan, conceived as a ghostly apparition to provoke fear but soon growing into a monster with many heads, which has since been often wounded but never slain. But with its ugly help the ballot was regained by the whites and denied to the blacks. Again the Negro was subdued and put back into servitude. Act One of the great racial drama was over. The curtain came down, and it was a long time before it came up again.

Meanwhile, the briefly liberated Negro, who had been led to expect a better life, soon found himself deserted by his former benefactors and stranded in a wasteland, his only hope and help for survival proffered by his old, but also helpless, master, in the risky business of sharecropping.

Unfair as it may have become, the sharecropping system was at first, and for a considerable time after the war, a necessity. The white man had the land, the Negro the strong back.

Neither had cash, capital, or commodities. Each was necessary for the other's survival. If the Negro was the bootstrap by which the Black Belt landowner lifted himself, the use of the land as a place to live and make a living was a life-raft for the Negro and also, it must not be forgotten, for the landless poor whites who became sharecroppers.

Farm operations were of necessity carried on by an elaborate system of credit: wholesale cotton buyers, called factors, borrowed money from New York bankers; the cotton factors in turn advanced sums to the farmer by taking mortgages on his prospective crop, sometimes on his land; the farmers advanced the sharecropper his provisions, seed, fertilizer, and hardware, and after harvest in the fall there was a reckoning all down the line. Unfortunately, by the time the farmer came to settle with his tenant, the tenant was wont to remark that the "deducts" got all the profits or left him deeper in debt.

It is undeniable that many farmers, hard-pressed to wring a living from this process, did take advantage of their tenants and farm hands. The landlords usually ran commissaries from which their tenants obtained the necessities of life on credit; and often, instead of money, the landlords issued a sort of personalized token-money called "brozenes," which could be spent only at their commissaries. Many tough-minded farmers charged exorbitant interest on incurred debts, were quick to close mortgages and sell out the debtor, mule, plow, wagon, even potatoes in his bank and the corn in his crib, thus bettering himself at the expense of tenants who could neither read, write, nor figure. Despite the system, however, a few sharecroppers who worked for honest landlords were able to survive and get ahead.

The farmer-merchant-landlord, though not to blame for the sharecropping system, must share the blame for perpetuating it. Inevitably, as the system proved more profitable for him, it became more difficult for him to abandon it. Because of the abundance of Negro labor and the landlord's preference for it, relatively few white sharecroppers remained in the Black Belt. Also, the cotton mills that came south did not settle in the

Black Belt, thus sparing it the problems of the mill towns with their child labor—white and often pellagrous children, called "lint-heads."

But the time eventually came when sharecropping became less profitable than cattle raising and timber farming; mechanical cultivation replaced the mule and plow, and many Negroes thus forced from the farms went unprepared to big cities in order to find employment. Many were lost in ghetto jungles, many went on welfare, but others found opportunities that had been denied them in the South, took advantage of these opportunities, and lifted themselves out of poverty and into a different and better world.

That the Negro has by no means been responsible for the position he has held in the Black Belt spectrum in the past, that he has been neglected, exploited, and discriminated against, even the most ungenerous whites now admit; but regardless of the divisiveness of the past decade, the good people of both races are trying to reach an understanding and a new respect. And if my observations and experience are correct, there is between many individuals and families of black and white real friendship, and between quite a number there is something deeper. It is appreciation and love.

True, the plight of rural blacks in the Black Belt is still depressing. Young blacks are not being taught the work skills they need in order to compete favorably with whites, and whites are still reluctant to admit them into many areas of the labor market. These handicaps for blacks not only depress the economy by putting more of them on the welfare rolls, but they induce the more talented and capable to go elsewhere where they can learn the needed skills to obtain the more lucrative jobs available to them. In consequence, the least able and least ambitious are the ones who are left behind.

But the lock has been broken and the gate is opening. Just how blacks have won the freedom to go anywhere, to do anything, to be somebody is, as we shall see later, what the second and third acts of the great racial drama of this century were all about.

FOURTEEN

The Tide Comes In

Midterm exams came and went. The air softened. It seemed that the hours inside the classroom would never end. Sap was rising. Bare branches turned pale coral, yellow, or green. Daffodils and jonquils popped up over night, defying the frosty mornings, and marched across the lawns, still winter-brown.

Spring was sure and near. Nature knew it. Man sensed it. Children especially were aware. The washed air smelled clean and sweet, the robins and red birds returned, doves cooed across hedgerows and bobwhites called across the meadows. Everything seemed touched with the heavenly. And why not? It was the ancient miracle of resurrection.

Came plowing time and then time for planting. Farm boys had to stay home from school to help. Others wished they might have been so lucky. The youngsters buzzed and hummed like a hive of bees preparing to swarm, their fingers itching to dig bait, cut willow whistles, and fashion sleek new slingshots; their feet fidgeting to be released from their leather cells; their minds restive and unattentive, wandering to hillsides, creek banks, and swimming holes.

Luckily for them there would be an hour or two between school and nightly chores for grubbing bare toes into damp creek banks, for dangling a worm before flicking minnows, for gathering wild honeysuckle or sweet shrubs to bring to their teacher next morning.

Even through the dust-streaked windowpanes one could see, mostly feel, life resurging. Neither brick walls nor sooty panes, frozen hearts, nor death itself could deny Nature's perennial flood tide. Only the tombstone angels and the old Confederate soldier in the cemetery across the way remained cold and unknowing.

In other ways a wan smile was flickering across the land in this spring of '34. Dollars had finally trickled down from the great white throne in Washington into the pockets of the man with the hoe, who, though leaning on his hoe more than he ought, nevertheless ate bread by day and slept less fearful by night. The farmer, though grumbling about the crowd in Washington being as crazy as loons for ordering pigs to be slaughtered and cotton plowed up, was reassured by a floor under his cash crops and cheap government loans to tide him over. Hope came also to the young, who, lifted out of vagrancy and aimless wandering, were clothed, sheltered and fed in C.C.C. Camps and paid for their labor and regimentation. And the Negro, who had survived on rabbit stew and collard greens, was given another chance. He could now have his forty acres and a mule, but only by signing up for forty years in which to pay for them. Grumbling there was to be sure, the everlasting companion of change; but there was hope, too, and where hope is, the heart does not faint.

After several feeble efforts, like a child testing its strength, spring burst out of its winding sheet with a barrage of magical sights and sounds and odors—which unless taken in broken doses could blind one to all common sense and duty.

You who have your blizzards or scorching winds, your rugged mountains or stark deserts to toughen your bodies, constrain your passions, and sharpen your wits, cannot understand what the shimmering, psychedelic springtimes and longer languorous summers can do for an animal, even though he be at the top of the ladder and call himself a man. It is no wonder that we are a bit daft, sentimental, tender of skin and tender of heart, with emotions lying only skin deep, as quick to love as to anger, both with equal intensity and unreasonableness. Nor is there any wonder that we are a hedonist lot of loafers and idlers, in a place where a voluptuous mistress strokes us with velvety fingers, lulling us with a siren's voice into wishful thinking and wanton living.

No doubt this spring was no lovelier than others. But to me it was. Perhaps I was more aware of it, for it had been some years since I had watched my homeland emerge from a dead chrysalis to stretch her wings. And perhaps it was because I was now experiencing a rebirth myself, leaving a world of mirages and frustrated dreams, and hopefully coming into a world of shared joy that promised to last a lifetime and beyond.

From afar one could see the brooding, somber hillsides softening and mottling under fresh veils of color—a misty, swirling study in greens—lime green, ice-blue green, avocado green, green of ocean spray, green of emeralds; clear cool greens, pale and tender; old warm greens, deep and strong. Nearer and proceeding with the days, red butterfly blossoms of the maples led the parade of flowering trees and shrubs: the vivid dashes of dogwood whites and of wild plum, grancy graybeard, and haws followed, along with the orchid of the Judas trees and soft pinks of crabs.

Closer to earth and nearer to man blossomed the shaded retiring things: the spidery pink and white honeysuckle, the fragrant yellow jasmine, white hydrangeas on ferny stream banks, and—hidden deep in cool canyons—clumps of mountain laurel and rhododendron. Then, almost underfoot, the tender, woodland plants; the small pale violet amid tiny ferns and mosses, the bolder, two-toned, bird-foot violets in brighter sun; the heart leaf with its fragrant leaves and its little-brown-jug blossoms; the sweet-shrub with its magenta blooms, whose fragrance increases in the warmth of a closed hand; and in their chosen soil, white and pink atamasco lilies, swamp iris, may apple, spiderwort, and others sprinkled over the forest floor.

As spring gave way to May, the rest of the world beyond the hills and woodland also came alive with beauty. Lining the roadsides and stretching away to hedgerows, acres of pasture land were painted with pink primrose cups and yellow dandelions, swatches of orchid sweet william, brown-eyed susans, purple vetches, crimson clovers, and hundreds of other small, bright-faced flowers. Trumpet vines and morning-glories decorated fences and the ubiquitous honeysuckle perfumed all the air that moved.

And in the town itself, where flowers were loved and fed

with hen-house and barnyard fertilizer, flower pits were opened and pots of ferns, geraniums, begonias, and night-blooming cereus were brought out and set in rows on porches, shelves, and steps. Front yards that had been brown stubble came alive and put on their Easter best. Pear, peach, crab, and apple trees shook out their white and pink umbrellas above the flowering shrubs underneath: snowy spiraea, syringa and deutsia, flowering quince, forsythia or butterfly bush, and the hardy bush roses. Ramblers, Van Fleets, Lady Banksia, and Marechal Neil roses transformed fences and trellises into things of beauty; while pergolas, porches, and arbors dripped with the grape-like clusters of wisteria. Then there were the little plants: violets, pansies, hyacinths, phlox, sweet alyssum, lantana and verbena. No flower in *Hastings* catalogue went overlooked or untried by these flower-loving people. (Only in recent years have azaleas and improved camellias dominated the southern garden.)

Nor did people in Camden confine themselves to the beautiful in their love of growing things. A large part of their care and attention was spent on the fragrant shrubs and plants which might have lovely blossoms or not. They loved the apple geranium, the heliotrope, Confederate Jasmine, tuberose, lilacs, and the spicy tea olive. Most pungent of all the fragrances were the bananalike odor of the small, almond-shaped blossoms of the magnolia-friscatta and the cloying sweetness of the hardy and then pestfree gardenias. In every yard grew the indestructible four-o'clock, whose delicate perfume remained locked in its blossoms until dusk. And somewhere near every house grew chinaberry and mimosa trees with their special sweetness in their blooming seasons.

All these fragrances drifted into open windows and doors, over palings and into paths and roadsides beyond. No heating or cooling systems then kept houses closed the year 'round, denying man the balm of gentle breezes and sweet odors and thereby dulling his instinctive seasonal rhythm with all living things, even with the universe itself.

Some people may have suffered more from allergies, but at

least they had nature's elixir to make their hearts leap up, to stir their bodies to romance, and to touch their minds with magic. They needed no drugs to lift them out of the humdrum and into a new dimension of awareness and delight. In fact, there often comes a time, when in the midst of a Southern spring's powerful, alluring spell, one feels constrained to wall off the profusion of beauty and to stoop in admiration before one tiny, tender flower, struggling up between bare rocks or binding roots, doing its best to brighten its small, hostile world. Such a sight gives one balance and perspective, causing one to smile and weep together, realizing that, not by over-powering bewitchment, but only by such small, personal gallantry can man, always alone and ever lonely, survive in this crazy world.

No wonder that during this dangerous time—of misty moons, warm suns, caressing airs, lacy shades—of birdsong by morning, fireflies by evening and whippoorwill's call by night, when Nature does her utmost to bring her earthlings into the mating season, Will and I decided to get married just as soon as the school term ended.

The decision came about after I had received a teaching contract for the following year. I mentioned the contract to Will, not by accident, and he responded as I hoped he would. He asked me not to sign it. He had other plans for me.

This was good news for me. I hoped it was for him. But, however it might turn out, he could never say that he had not been warned. His dwarflike handy man, Uncle Louie, had cautioned him. "Should you marry that lady," he had said, "you're gonna see a heap o' stars, and they ain't gonna be in heben." Uncle Louie was ancient as the hills and had been married longer than he could remember. He could have known something.

As for me, I felt I had much for which to thank the Good Lord. And I did.

FIFTEEN

A Shoal Passed

Summer came. School closed—much to the rejoicing of pupils as well as teachers. Having no money with which to buy a trousseau, I was forced to stitch up my own wedding dress and make do on whatever else my sisters could contribute.

On the sixth of June, 1934, Will Liddell and I were married. In such a happy circumstance I could, and did, believe that any apprehensions I might have had about Camden were nonsense; and that of all places on earth it was and would always be "my other Eden, my demi-paradise."

We set up housekeeping in what had been the Liddell home for forty years past. It was a big, two-story house built in 1847 for the huge sum of $4,750, now for some years having been occupied by Will, living alone except for his bird dogs, in two downstairs bedrooms. Bachelorlike, his interest in the house was limited to this small corner of the place. The rest of the interior was a shambles, and a wilderness surrounded it from without.

So large and empty was the house that it echoed to every voice and footfall as if it were a fathomless cave; so unsightly from disuse and neglect that no other member of the family wanted any part of it; so girded by bushes, vines, and trees growing wildly and at random that, with all of its fifty feet from ground to chimney top, it could not be seen from the street or gotten to except from the rear. But it did not leak, its heart-pine timbers, solid and secured by wooden pegs, were intact, and its four great chimneys had lost not a single brick.

Surveying the whole, I set my sights on a five-year plan for rehabilitating the place, a plan that turned into a lifetime project still not finished—nor will it ever be unless by some miracle-meeting of money and imagination and love of old things. But, by improvising and making do, the old house, with a little money and something approaching the twelve labors of

Hercules, finally became a home filled with the joys and pains of living, rather than a cavern filled with hollow echoes.

Although the faded wallpaper hung in strips from the ceilings, fourteen feet high; though the eight-by-five windows glared unblinking through shredded curtains, if any; though the two great halls reverberated like the haunts of spooks; though the eight cavernous fireplaces gaped like toothless mouths in the sixteen-by-eighteen-foot rooms—with eight bare mantels above them—and though the uncarpeted stairs stretched up like a ladder to the moon and a veritable jungle closed in from without, I was undismayed by so vast a renovation project. In fact, at the time, the place posed no problems at all. I was happy, and I felt safe and secure at last. Nothing else mattered.

However, long before I had rugs on the floors, paper on the walls, or shades at the windows, an old friend of the Liddell family paid me a visit, and in confidential mood told me of an incident concerning Will and myself before we were married—she thinking, no doubt, that it would be amusing to me, since any danger it might have posed for our marriage was then passed. I must admit, however, that it was very unfunny then and still is to this good day.

It so happened that at the very time I was so hopeful and happy at the prospects of getting myself a husband and a home, there was considerable anxiety among some of the pillars of the Presbyterian Church about the seemingly serious trend of our romance and its possible consequences, so much so that these friends decided that some action should be taken. First they prayed over the matter; not receiving any clear directive from on high, they then consulted the pastor of the flock about what should be done and how best to proceed.

It seems that the concern was not so much for me as for Will, who, being a deacon at the time, could well jeopardize his standing in the church and commit an unorthodox indiscretion if he married a divorcée. Being serious Bible students and believing its admonitions to be infallible and final, these friends felt that they could not stand by silently as one of their deacons, and a dear friend besides, involved himself in a situation so compromising as those described in Mark 10:12 and the last portion of Matthew 5:32. In the one case I would become an adultress on remarriage, and in the other Will would become an adulterer if he married me. What a fine kettle of fish these verses must have presented to these good people! And I and my predicament entirely to blame.

It is easy to see why these statements in Scripture have been stumbling blocks for Christians for centuries, and why some faiths still hold them morally inviolable. I could also understand the great concern of these people for Will's welfare, but understanding the clout did not diminish its impact on my head. Innocently enough, I had supposed that the Presbyterian Church had made its peace with this fact of life. Maybe the church had, but its individual members evidently had not.

The strange solution of this problem, one that may have cleared our path to the altar, came about through the aid of the minister to whom these disturbed ones came—a Dr. Campbell, a native of Scotland and as orthodox a man as was likely to be found at this time and in this place. Fortunately, Dr. Campbell took the problem under consideration and in due time offered his counsel and advice.

It is difficult to say why old Dr. Campbell ruled in our favor—he was seemingly a most unlikely judge to rule for such clemency—except that he was apparently estranged from his wife and may have yearned for a freedom he dared not attempt to legalize. Nevertheless, his argument on my behalf, though clearing me on the one hand, practically damned me on the other. His defense was that, if I had been sinned against rather than sinning in the dissolution of my marriage (as might be ascertained by examining the divorce decree), then it could be assumed that the marriage had never existed. (Just how this could be assumed without condemning me for living in sin during those years was difficult to grasp.) But in assuming this premise, the stumbling block would be removed and the way cleared for Will to marry me without transgressing.

Evidently this reasoning was either acceptable or too involved to be questioned. At any rate, nothing was done to
disturb our plans to be married. But for years afterward,
whenever I happened upon these two verses of Scripture, I
cringed and felt like crawling under the carpet. Unfortunately,
I was one of those souls who already felt burdened with guilt
complexes galore, and this only added another big rock to my
load.

For old Dr. Campbell's aid, however, and his further willingness to marry Will and me, I will ever be grateful. He won
for himself an ardent admirer and an attentive listener to his
repetitious and rambling sermons, which invariably put a
goodly number of his congregation to sleep every Sunday
morning.

Considering how another resolution of this matter might
have altered the course of my life, surely for the worse, my
uneasiness about Camden returned. I had been warned, but I
had not believed that my past could be such a threat to my
future. But if the past could not be cast off, then it must be
lived with. Heaven be praised, I was safely married when I
became informed of this now-past danger. But the knowledge
of it made me again feel ill at ease.

Will knew nothing about this brush with fate until many
years later, when I finally got up courage to mention it. Silence
had not been golden in this instance. It was merely an effort on
my part to bury this unhappy image, which my past had evidently painted in at least a few minds. When I did recount the
episode, the answer I got was probably what I might have
received had I mentioned it to start with. "Nothing came of it,"
he said. "So what?"

SIXTEEN

We Go to Church on Sunday

Camden has always been a church-going and a church-loving community. The Liddell family went. They always had. Now being one of them, I would go too. No question or argument about that.

The small Camden Presbyterian Church, U.S., built in 1885, after fire destroyed an earlier structure built in 1845, was dignified, architecturally sound, simple and pleasant to the eye. The building stood as originally constructed when I came to Camden in 1933. There was a double entrance into the vestibule, a belfry with a bell that had a happy tone, above which the steeple did its part by pointing people to heaven. The lancet windows were tall, arched, and shuttered inside with small-paneled blinds. The pews were graceful, the floors made of wide-boarded, mellowed pine; two coal-burning stoves heated it and a pump organ furnished the music. There was no Sunday School building. All classes met at once in the sanctuary and, while proceeding, sounded like the Tower of Babel.

There was one odd feature of the interior, one which provoked either praise or distaste according to the beholder's eye. It was a vista painted across the entire rear wall—shadowed columns flanking a parquet floor, receding to a far-off door, giving the impression of a spacious corridor with an exit to somewhere beyond. It was said that an itinerant sign painter had come through Camden as the church was being completed and that the painting was done at his suggestion. Whether it was compatible with a worshipful spirit was debatable. It looked more like a Roman forum than a church extension, but was, nevertheless, intriguing.

Strangely enough, this painting had some unhappy effects on imaginative youngsters as they perforce had to contemplate it during long, tedious sermons hardly fashioned to entertain them. Will Liddell admitted that as a boy he thought that beyond the far-off door, there was a room full of snakes to which a boy might be consigned if he didn't behave himself in church. Our son confessed that he thought the devil lived back there, waiting to snatch bad people and take them to the bad place.

Maybe we could use some such coercion nowadays to restrain youngsters who believe in neither hell nor the devil. But the old painting was lost in the course of remodeling, as were the stoves, the hanging lamps, and the pump organ. There was one sad loss, as usually occurs when new things replace old; the windows, which used to be thrown open to catch the breezes and let in the light, and through which one might glimpse the leaves fluttering or the clouds drifting by, now stay shut the year round, with shutters tightly closed. Does this, perhaps convey something about our little cocooned church? Why couldn't we, in springtime at least, open the windows and let the soft fragrant air and the sunshine pour in, adding a fillip to the weekly rubbing and scrubbing the minister gives us?

Of all Southern Presbyterian churches, few, if any, have changed less from its more-than-century-old fundamentalist stand on Scripture and church doctrine than the Camden Church. The members like it this way. Consequently, in recent years it has been well nigh impossible to find a minister conservative enough to suit us. For years the church was served by a retired minister or students still in the seminary. I sympathized with these dedicated young men, having to cut their wisdom teeth on our rigidly set congregation. By the time they left us their halos must have been knocked pretty cockeyed, but they had no doubt acquired heads full of hard sense that served them well elsewhere.

Though old Dr. Campbell was minister when I arrived in Camden, the thinking, if not the action, of the church was molded by several maiden ladies whose mission in life was to teach the Bible wherever and whenever a group could be gotten together—little, big, old or young. Into our noggins they poured in and pressed down, line upon line, precept upon precept, what Presbyterians were supposed to believe, exactly as they had been taught at the Moody Bible Institute. The imprint of their teaching on their survivors is pronounced to this good day.

I might have been happier had I not learned so much from them, for of all my conflicts with life in Camden, my efforts to reconcile what I did believe with what I was told I should believe were the most frustrating. I felt as if I were set to wandering barefoot through a prickly pear patch. Possibly my basic problem was that I was not a fundamentalist; hence there was no firm meeting ground for a mind believing Scripture to be God's infallible word and one believing that God did not use the men who wrote the Bible as dictaphones—thereby allowing them the probability of error in fact or in judgment colored by their knowledge, their inherited beliefs, or the exigencies in which they found themselves. Although such interpretation gives me, as it gives others, considerable consolation, it nevertheless opens a Pandora's box for the orthodox, the escaping ideas appearing as stumbling blocks in the pathway to truth.

Never having been grounded in Presbyterian doctrine, except in the catechism, as a child (most of which I did not understand), I was perplexed by many questions these Bible teachers raised: how to reconcile predestination with free will; how to explain election (before the foundation of the world) of those to be saved and those to be damned; how to reconcile an unchanging God with the history of His dealings with His people, or the God of vengeance and wrath of the Old Testament with the God of love and mercy in the New. (Presbyterians explain this by God's dispensations, first of law and then of grace.) How to accept the belief that whatever comes to pass is either with God's permission or according to His will. And other hard doctrine, hard for me. Such quicksand questions are dangerous enough for theologians, and minds of lesser light might best leave them alone, or turn them over to the Good Lord himself as some of His mysteries not meant to be understood by mere man.

To interpret any of the Old Testament stories as symbolism

or allegory was dangerous indeed. To doubt the literal interpretation of one would jeopardize the truth of all. And a good Presbyterian was supposed to "know" many, many things about faith and doctrine. He could not afford to just "believe." He must know. Among other things, that he was saved—no ifs, ands, or buts. For questions of doubters or differers, Scripture was quoted as the answer and final proof, leaving the not-so-sure still not so sure. Many a time I felt that attempting to squeeze this mystical, magical thing called religion into formulated statements, no matter how profound, was like trying to put a rainbow into a bottle.

Trying to reconcile my questing and often disturbed conscience with some of our harsh and dour Calvinistic teachings was, through the years, a lonely battle for me. And sometimes a losing one. But as time marched on, even the Camden Presbyterian Church softened its stand on many matters; and besides becoming more conservative myself, I began to realize that others also deviated in their thinking and yet were admittedly Christian, even Presbyterian. Also, that differing with each other was nothing new. It had always been that way, else there would be no Presbyterian Church. (Even today hundreds of our conservative sister churches are breaking away from the mother church, which has become too liberal in its thinking for them.)

Finally I became assured that, since believing as I did undergirded my faith rather than weakening it, it was perhaps good for me. I was willing to have others believe as they must. Might I not yield the same privilege to myself? God, not man, must eventually judge us all, and I would have to take my chances with Him. I, with others, can be everlastingly thankful for the blueprint that the Creator has left us for living our lives and saving our souls, one in which even the least of us can find comfort, communion, and comprehension. Whether one follows this Master Plan or one of his own choosing must, surely, determine his destiny, here and hereafter.

Will's faith was a different matter. It was sure, simple, and uncluttered with dogma or doctrine. He came by it from long association with the real thing, not from struggling with or pondering the whys of what someone else or even the Bible said. It was a happy, ingrafted part of him, and he never disturbed it with the probe of argument, question, or doubt. In this, I continually envied him.

But it did seem that these ardent maiden ladies of the church, one of whom still believed in infant damnation—a belief we mothers would have none of, regardless of her "proofs" from Scripture—were sublimating their frustrations born of spinsterhood by attempting to subjugate us married women to the complete domination of our husbands. They could well afford to admonish us continually with certain Biblical pronouncements such as: "Thy desire shall be to thy husband and he shall rule over thee," or "Let the women keep silent in the church——and if they will learn anything, let them ask their husbands at home," and "Neither was man created for woman, but woman for man," and "Let the woman learn in silence with all subjection—nor usurp authority over the man," and "Wives, submit yourselves to your husbands,"—that a wife should adorn herself "in modest apparel and be grave, sober, and faithful in all things." They further admonished the deacons and elders to be ones "that ruleth well their own houses."

Alas and alack, Bible or no Bible, it was already too late for such advice. Women were voting and drinking, smoking and swearing, bobbing their hair and wearing their skirts up to their knees; and their husbands were hardly allowed to rule themselves, much less their households.

Dr. Campbell was still minister of our church when time came to christen our first-born. The experience was one not easily forgot. Never before nor since have I heard the exact ceremony Dr. Campbell used that morning. As we stood before the altar, holding our six-month-old son, as angelic as parents could wish, the rather detailed meaning of the service was read. Then, before the act of christening, certain questions were put to Will and me as parents. It was the first, however, which so dumfounded me that I heard little or nothing thereafter:

"Do you, as parents, confess and agree that this child was conceived in sin and that his heart is above all things desperately wicked?"

My mind stood still. The thought, a thousand times quicker than the tongue, wanted to scream "No!" to both questions. The child was *not* conceived in sin, not according to *my* book. And his heart was not desperately wicked! But there is one thing you can always count on from a Presbyterian—he'd much prefer being wrong than rude, so I did as was expected of me. I nodded assent.

But all the way home I jumped up and down like the lid on a thumping tea kettle, taking the preacher to task for asking us such a question. But Will reacted as he always did when I was in a dither. He said nothing, nothing at all. When we got home, he lifted the coverlet from his peacefully sleeping son and looked him over. "I think he'll live," he said, ending the matter. And then I reacted as usual by getting furious with Will for not getting angry along with me.

Strangely enough, after a long time and a lot of living and watching others live, I, too, am convinced of original sin. In fact, I'm convinced of sin—original, ever-present, and everlasting. I now feel more charitable about Dr. Campbell's christening service. But I am glad that that form has been abandoned.

Another time, during World War II, when V-bombs were devastating England, one of these maiden teachers remarked that the sanctuary should never be used for anything other than worship. I suggested that were we bombed, it might well be used for a temporary hospital. The reply was, "Not as long as there is some other place." Again I boiled over, violently disagreeing with this attitude of not using the church building for acts of mercy. Will's answer to me and to the problem was plain and to the point. "If we were bombed," he said, "we'd use the church and not ask this good lady's permission." This time his answer did satisfy me. There were men in the church after all. They might not say much, but they could be counted on to act when the chips were down.

But it must be said, to the everlasting praise of these dedicated women, that they held the church together through years of decline, and gave their pupils a knowledge of the Bible that was invaluable both as instruction and inspiration. Furthermore, they went out among our Negroes and did missionary work, which we fail to do today. Also they aided, by their generosity and encouragement, many young white boys and girls to enter careers that would have been otherwise unattainable and thereby helped them to become successful citizens. These, particularly, have not forgotten their benefactors, and they bless them to this day.

Until recently an annual revival, held in mid- or late summer, was considered a necessary spiritual injection to arouse the lethargic congregation and to "bring in" some souls sadly in need of salvation, who in turn were sadly needed by the church to sustain its membership. Before air-conditioning, hand fans—palmetto, Japanese silk, accordion-folding, but most often the pasteboard kind with a picture of Jesus on one side and "Compliments of Albritton Drug Store" on the other—went like metronomes throughout the service to combat the heat; preachers were invited to visit around and all but foundered on fried chicken, chicken pie, garden vegetables, and hand-turned ice cream. But because Presbyterians were so little aroused and so few sinners were saved, these meetings, if held at all, have declined into Bible lectures.

The really rip-snortin' revivals of the not-too-distant past, which Presbyterians generally frowned upon, were the camp meetings held in woodland areas, conducted in tents by itinerant preachers. In some ways these revivals resembled, on a small scale, the modern rock festivals, minus pot and nudity. People came from all over, loaded down with provisions as if for a siege, pitched tents, or lived in cabins on the campground.

Here one might witness the fire-and-brimstone preaching of the sulfurous old-time religion, liberally sprinkled with "Amens" and "Hallelujahs"; the shouting and swooning of candidates as they "came through," the stuffing of skinny kids and fat old folks with fried catfish, barbecued pork, light bread, and layer cake, served on rough wooden tables but still called "dinner on the ground." There was weak lemonade by the lardcanful, with plenty of alcoholic beverages on the side, either from a pint in the pocket or a jug in the bushes.

So wrought up did people become at times that a sort of mass hysteria would prevail, with manifestations of being filled with the Holy Spirit; fainting fits, shouting, crying out, speaking in tongues, and confessing to sins probably never committed or to others best left dead and buried. Such a sin, confessed to by an overly penitent woman who declared that her child had not been fathered by her husband, caused the husband to denounce her as the Devil's handmaiden and to order her to go immediately to the latter's abode.

Between preachings and prayer meetings there was said to be no dearth of "extracurricular" activity, particularly after nightfall. As one observer put it, "For every soul the Lord saved, the Devil created two." But with all their emotional frenzy, these meetings served a need, a need for a lively vacation as well as a purging and cleansing, which, like a course of calomel, cured many a patient just because he thought it did.

We can be thankful that the ruling elders no longer turn people out of the church or reprimand them as they once did. Maybe members became too scarce and hard to come by. But in the early 1900s it was no extraordinary procedure to "church" members for such minor sins as public profanity, indecent dancing, playing cards, drunkenness, or traveling on the Sabbath Day. Whatever the indiscretion, apology and repentance were demanded as the price of reinstatement. Other churches, however, profited by this ruling by readily taking in those who kicked over the traces and then refused to return to the fold.

Through the years we have often repeated over the dinner table some of the funny things that have occurred in our little churches in Camden.

There was Brother Robinson, for instance, pastor of the Associate Reform Presbyterian Church, who had a habit while preaching of leaning back, thrusting his hands into his pockets, then swaying back and forth until his point was made, only to repeat when the next point of emphasis arrived. His wife begged him to stop this annoying habit, but he seemed unable to do so. Determined to cure him, she sewed up his pockets one Sunday morning. Never was Brother Robinson nearer hell than during the ensuing half-hour in the pulpit, suffering through the futile reaching for pockets and not finding them there, his bewildered confusion, and the disorganized sermon that followed. Before it was all over, Mrs. Robinson, as humiliated as her spouse, concluded that her cure had been worse then the disease, and ripped the pockets open, never again to attempt a remedy.

There was the baptismal service at the Baptist church while Brother Roark was pastor there. When the ceremony began, the organist started playing and continued to play throughout, with trills and variations, the hymn, "Oh, Happy Day." Certain eyebrows went up, while smiles flickered across the congregation. As Brother Roark, solemnly unaware of the connection, was giving his candidates for church membership a very damp time, some not-too-reverent members of the congregation were translating "Oh, Happy Day" into its barroom version, "How dry I am, how dry I am; nobody knows how dry I am."

On another occasion this hymn caused a certain funeral to be something less than sad and gloomy. A particular Walter Mitty sort of husband, liberated by the death of his long-time, henpecking helpmeet, requested that the funeral music include "Oh, Happy Day." The organist obliged and the congregation approved, even if their satisfaction was difficult to conceal.

There was Brother Dannelly, a preacher at the Methodist church, who, in a surge of eloquence, spat out his false teeth. But, good catch that he was, he retrieved them in mid-air, pocketed them without ado, and never missed a lick of his sermon. And his congregation, chivalrous to the core, never let on that they were aware.

One summer our Presbyterian church employed an assistant minister who lived in our home. Hearing him express a desire to go horseback riding, our daughter took him to the plantation one Saturday afternoon and gave him a cow-horse, the only one available, to ride. They rode down a familiar pasture road; and the boy, trying to keep up, kicked the old horse sharply in the ribs. When the horse began to lope off too rapidly for comfort, his rider reined him in as tightly as possible in an effort to hold him down.

Unfortunately, this movement happened to be a cow-driver's signal to take off hell-for-leather after a steer, which is what the horse did. But coming to an abrupt turn in the road, the horse took the turn leading to the barn, while the boy went straight ahead, landing seat-side down in the middle of the graveled road.

Not to be outdone, he caught the horse and tried again. The same thing happened, except that the old horse opened up down the public road, across a high bridge over a deep slough, with his rider holding onto the pommel of the saddle for dear life, his feet flying out like paddles. Some people passing in a car saw the boy's predicament, got out and waved the horse to a sudden stop. Again the young fellow went flying over the horse's head, this time into the bushes.

Needless to say, he was in a painful condition. By Sunday morning he could hardly sit, rise, or stand. He had Will tape up his raw backside before going to church, carried a pillow into the pulpit for easing his sitting, and haltingly rose to read the Scripture as chosen by the minister for his sermon. It was taken from Psalm 139, portions of which were: "The Lord knoweth my down-sitting and my up-rising . . . Thou hast beset me behind and before . . ."

Roy Liddell, Will's oldest brother and as proper a church elder as could be imagined, once assumed the duty of introducing a newcomer to the congregation, the newcomer's name being Baty, pronounced with a short "a." The two rose, Roy warmly welcomed his companion and, after a frantic moment of searching his memory for the name, came up with "Mister Nutty."

This recalls something that happened to Preacher Hill of the Methodist church. He was invited by one of his parishioners, Mrs. Claude Bryant, for Sunday dinner. In preparing the meal, Mrs. Bryant had chosen kid, of rather dubious age, for her main dish. She kept telling herself that she must put on her best company manners and be sure to call the meat "kid" and not "goat," as she might have called it under different circumstances. Sure enough, so intent was she on saying the proper thing, that when the platter of meat was passed to Preacher Hill, she came out with "Won't you have some kid, Brother Goat?"

An accomplished vocalist, Willela Burford, was asked, soon after her arrival in Camden as a bride, to sing a solo in the Baptist church. As the song went along, Willela saw flickers of amusement flashing across the congregation, which upset her considerably, making her wonder whether she was singing off key or if her petticoat were falling off. After services she learned the reason for the congregation's smiles. Everyone wanted to know if she really meant what she had sung over and over with each refrain, "I will arise and go, back to my Father and home."

Our churches and their services are dignified and reverential, none more so than the Presbyterian. We were aghast a while back when we learned how a group of young people of our own denomination had conducted a communion service. To use an expression of their own, they went ape, by playing rock music in the sanctuary, marching with placards on one of which was blazoned "Sock it to us, Jesus!"; by serving communion while dressed in jeans and sandals, drinking sacramental wine from a tin pitcher, biting bread from a loaf of bakery bread, and singing the Lord's Prayer to the tune of "Waltzing Matilda."

This was an isolated incident, but some oldsters are shocked

by such mild innovations as singing songs other than hymns in the church, *and* to guitar accompaniment rather than organ. Recently, even I turned a bit queasy when in a Christmas pageant one of the young people read: "And Joseph went up
from Galilee . . . to be taxed with Mary his fiancée in her last days of pregnancy." The preacher better bring some smelling salts along when he reads from the *Good News Bible,* instead of "Adam knew Eve," that "Adam and Eve had intercourse."

(After the initial shock, such plain English might be invigorating; but why the watered-down, kindergarten language of much of these new Bibles? Reading them compared to reading the King James version is like drinking whey instead of wine. These modern translators must think they have to use weak, insipid language in order to reach weak, insipid souls. In my opinion, a dose of lofty passages from the old Bible might better inspire these souls to "Lift up their eyes unto the hills.")

In our local church, integration is not now a matter of concern. This might seem strange in view of the church's past, when it was considered a duty to teach slaves the Christian faith. Slaves went to church with their masters, although segregated, usually seated in a balcony set aside especially for them. If no church was accessible, they were taught Bible lessons in the kitchen of the big house in inclement weather, outside under shade trees in fair.

After the Civil War, Negroes established their own churches, usually with the support and under the auspices of Northern denominations. During the postwar era, white Southern churches shifted their mission work largely to foreign fields, leaving the work among our own Negroes to Northern churches, which did a splendid work in Wilcox County in connection with the mission schools they established here.

Our Camden church, at long last, was actively mending fences and making progress in home-mission work among the black people when the civil-rights movement exploded like a bombshell right on top of us. For several years prior to this turmoil and during its duration, civil-rights workers swarmed

93

in, many of them preachers, all using the Negro churches for living quarters from which freedom marches and demonstrations were organized and launched. These civil-rights workers were treated with contempt, hostility, and (in some cases) even violence by the whites; the Negro churches were equally vilified for their complicity.

With a thorny hedge grown up between the two church communities, our local whites either did not care, or did not dare, to visit the Negro churches for fear of ostracism or social stigma. But that condition has changed for the better. Occasionally a few whites do go to the Negro churches, and in regional gatherings representatives of both races meet each other with kindness and cordiality. Integration of our local Presbyterian church would be adamantly opposed, but the question has not yet arisen; the Negroes with whom I am acquainted tell me that they prefer their own churches, where they can worship as they please. They now have attractive new or renovated churches of which they are very proud.

But our mother church, formed in the anguish of the Civil War, is torn by schism. Our local church felt that it was becoming too liberal, that it was considering union with the Northern Presbyterians, and that it was slipping a step here and a step there from the fundamentalist interpretation of the Scripture. Therefore, it was not surprising that in 1975 it withdrew from the mother church and joined the Presbyterian Church of America, a dissenting group already withdrawn.

Will's comments about leaving the old church were largely sentimental. "I was born into this church eighty years ago," he said, "and now it's not mine anymore." But he was wrong. He sits in the same pew, sings the same songs, and says the same prayers. He is his own church. He carries it around in his heart.

I hated to leave the old church for sentimental reasons also, and I felt that in withdrawing from it we were taking a step back into stricter fundamentalism, a direction I did not prefer. But I do not always agree with things I love: family, friends, church, or country. Nor do I expect them to always agree with me. My church has always been a thing of love in my life, and it always will be.

Many times the frail little bark has seemed to be a "painted ship upon a painted ocean," rudderless and becalmed; but each time a new generation has come aboard, taken her helm, and hoisted sail again.

Only God can read the future, but man can read the past. Throughout the years the little country church has been for its own "a refuge and strength, a very present help in time of trouble." It has nurtured our spirits, championed the eternal verities and nobler virtues, and pointed out the high road in a tumultuous and depraved world.

Here in her arms we have seen our babies christened, our children taught and guided, our young sons and daughters married. Often beset, our lives have been undergirded, fortified, and calmed. Here we have communed, here said our prayers of need and praise and thanksgiving; here we have bidden our friends and family members farewell in their brief pause on their last journey to the grave. And here we envisage our own leave-taking as we, too, must follow.

Acknowledging her failures and shortcomings, we still feel our church to be a hallowed place, and we who have been blessed by her would wish to keep it so.

SEVENTEEN

Killed with Kindness

In the years of the Great Depression and until recently sophisticated and skeptical times, Camden people did themselves to death with kindness. They still do, almost.

One night soon after my arrival in Camden, I brought up the rear of a long line at the ticket window of the movie theater. Mister Bagget, the owner and manager, smiled and told me that he was sorry, but he had only standing room left, to which

I was, of course, welcome free of charge. The picture had shown for the last three days and nights, so I couldn't understand how the house could be full when the entire population would scarcely have filled it three times. "There'd be plenty of room," Mr. Bagget said, "but the house is full of free-seaters tonight."

"Free-seaters?" I inquired, not understanding.

"Yes," he explained, "it's this way. When anyone sees a picture once, he feels he's entitled to see it free as many times thereafter as he wishes. This happens to be one of those pictures most folks like to see over and over again."

I could not refrain from remarking that the lack of consideration on the part of his patrons hardly justified his generosity.

"I know," he said. "But they patronize me pretty well, and when I have a slim crowd I don't mind. I don't mind the free-seaters so much," he continued, "as the ones who go in on half fare when they should be paying whole."

"And your vocabulary doesn't contain the word 'No'?" I suggested.

"They're all my friends," he explained, "and there are certain things one doesn't say to friends, and they know it."

"But when do these people admit that they are grown?"

"Oh, when they get married and have kids of their own, they sort of get convinced of it," he chuckled.

I had no argument or advice for anyone who held his public in such high regard.

Sadly, the old picture theater with its harmless heroine-swooning, pie-slinging, gun-smoking, cop-chasing cinemas, under whose spell so many, young and old, spent so many happy hours, has closed its doors in Camden, a casualty of an integration that would not be tolerated. However, what with most movies gone sick or sadistic, maybe we are lucky not to have a theater anymore.

For many years the water meters were never read and everyone used as much water as he could and wasted as much as he wished, receiving an unvarying bill of miniscule proportions, which if ever paid at all was paid because one was in the habit of doing that sort of thing. After the overwhelming reform of meter reading came about, I was shocked to see my two-fifty bill rocket up to ten dollars. But when I took it down, complaining that it "looked too big," it was reduced to what I considered a reasonable size. Upon honest reflection, however, I did wonder if watering a vegetable and a flower garden during a drought might not have had something to do with the size of the bill.

One old Camden resident was dead set against paying for such a common commodity as water. He was like Captain Charley Locklin, an old riverboat captain, who on retiring, moved to Mobile. Deciding the city was no place for him, he promptly returned. "I'll be damned," he said, "if I'll live anywhere where I have to pay for wood and water." The stubborn old Camden citizen, however, wouldn't move away or die, so eventually in a fit of reform, the town council voted to cut his water off. He had an invalid wife, and on her behalf an emotional backlash went into motion, and the town fathers were forced to rescind their action and to furnish free water to the old fellow for as long as his wife lived. As it turned out, she outlived him by many years.

Nowadays, with meters haphazardly read, most complaints are still settled under the prevailing notion that a customer's judgment, if not more accurate, is at least more important than a meter's.

Electricity problems, until the midfifties, when the Alabama Power Company bought out the Liddell Power Plant, were treated similarly. When I married into the Liddell family, no one, no matter how delinquent in paying his bills, was ever cut off. What a satisfaction to know that the steak would get done and the ice cream frozen, and that the lamp would still light, whether the light bill was paid or not.

"Why not try cutting these folks off for a change?" I suggested, since money was a mighty scarce article in our house about that time.

"It's bad business," Will answered. "We cut off a few folks

once and they didn't speak to us for five years. Anyway," he added, "they're our friends."

Through the years when we couldn't do this or buy that, I played that old tune over, but it never had the least effect on Will. He definitely preferred his friends to a paid-up bill. And now that the picture is whole, I know that he was right.

Instead of "let the buyer beware," the slogan for Camden was then, and still is, "let the seller beware." One could charge anything until crops were gathered, and if there were no crops, then a charge would be carried on and on until any purchase was worn out and a good riddance if the merchant wanted it back. Whatever his intentions about paying, a buyer could rest assured that no bill collector would beat his door down and that no moving van would cart off his unpaid-for movables.

Furthermore, if a customer wasn't satisfied, the merchant might hem and haw about compensation, but he always came around, especially where a woman was concerned. When dressed, sto'-bought turkeys were considered quite a deluxe item; one day a customer found, after she took her Thanksgiving turkey home, that it still contained the craw. In a huff, the lady took the craw back to the grocer and demanded that he weigh it and deduct twenty cents per pound from the price of the bird. "I refuse to pay twenty cents a pound for corn," she announced. Needless to say, the grocer bought back his nickel's worth of corn.

It is still mentioned how a tender-hearted banker of Camden lost loans to friends and other folks in need, and how this or that merchant went broke by crediting his friends—who included everybody—most of whom might have, but did not see fit to pay their accounts. Doctors doctored for a thank-you or for a gallon of syrup or a peck of potatoes, lawyers practiced likewise, and their debtors were more likely to be those driving white horses and drinking bourbon than those dipping snuff and driving a team of oxen. One just couldn't be so rude as to question a gentleman's intent or, equally insulting, his ability to pay his debts. A debt, like a man's mistress, simply was not a matter to be mentioned.

Probably no one so willingly knocked themselves out with kindness as did Miss Marguerite Jones and Miss "Snooks" Bailey during the days when they were the phone company's two "Centrals," night and day. Besides keeping all of Camden's watches and clocks synchronized, they were the town's information bureau and fire alarm.

When someone wanted the doctor and he wasn't in, Central was supposed to know where he was and usually did. In fact, he often left word with Central of his whereabouts. If a parent or child was out too late or too long, Central could be counted on to locate the tardy one. Not wishing to play second fiddle to another, a boy would call in to find out if a particular girl had a date before attempting to make one for himself. People wanting to hitch rides, cars being scarce, found out from Central who was going where, and when.

Central's desk was close by a window overlooking the main street, and a common request was to "please look out the window and see if so-and-so is on the street or on the loafer's bench on the court house lawn." Or "please send word to Tuck's drugstore (downstairs), and have them send out a mustard plaster for Grandpa or a bottle of cough syrup for little Jennie."

And when a fire alarm was phoned in, Central stuck her head out the window, rang a dinner bell, and yelled "Fire! at so-or-so's house," at the top of her lungs. Immediately all able-bodied men dropped whatever they were doing, grabbed available fire extinguishers and buckets, piled into whatever cars were on the street—nobody ever thought of locking a car or taking keys out—tore out to the fire, formed a bucket brigade and, with water from a garden hose (if lucky) or a well (if not), put out more fires than not. Usually by the time the fire was out, however, everything inside had been dashed out of doors and windows unless, of course, some dunce had jammed a worthless piano in the front door and a cookstove in the back—thereby saving some of what might have otherwise been splintered to bits.

Occasionally Central got cussed out for being so long making connections, but whoever did such a thing didn't realize how busy she was keeping people informed of births, deaths, or how the sick were progressing by the hour. Only once did I ever hear that she lost her cool. One night a man wanting to notify kinfolks of his father's death made a dozen calls scattered from New York to San Francisco. Wrong numbers, wrong names—the calls were the very dickens to get through. Finally, exhausted, Central stretched out to catch a wink of sleep before daylight, when the same man called in to say he had to make all the calls over again—his father had not died after all. "Next time you keep me up all night like this," Central told him, "you better be damn sure your daddy's dead."

Our first child was born at home early on a Sunday morning. By nightfall all the kinfolks had visited the new baby, and thereafter for two weeks the friends came, bringing gifts and goodies. Birthing a baby in Camden, I discovered, was a minor matter compared to entertaining the visitors. There was hardly time those first days to feed the baby or change his diapers. When the waves of kindness receded, I swore, and I kept the promise, never to have another baby in Camden. Next time I went to Selma, thirty miles distant, but still not far enough away to get the rest that I coveted as pay for my trouble.

The same sort of treatment is bestowed on a bride—friends and relatives outdoing themselves with parties, teas, showers, and then the traditional wedding with rehearsal party and reception. And Camden expects the wedding with all the trimmings; but woe to the bride who overlooks a certain friend or acquaintance in her invitations, and woe to the friend who hasn't a darn good reason for not attending.

At the turn of the century a very unkind thing was done at weddings, and done by the bride herself to her friends. The wedding presents were displayed with cards designating not only the donors but the amounts paid for each gift. What curious eying of these price tags there must have been and what clucking and tish-tishing as comparisons were made.

Later these tags were eliminated and, thankfully, in recent years even names of the donors are removed.

Nowadays, when the write-ups of these weddings, whether fifty-dollar or five-thousand-dollar variety, come out in the paper they all sound much alike. During the forties and fifties however, "the sweetly solemn ceremony took place before an altar of gracefully festooned smilax, banked with plumosa fern and standards of regal lilies [or gladioli and mums], while the delectable scene was softly lighted by tiers of gleaming cathedral tapers." The Titian (or brunette) beauty of the bride was always exquisitely gowned in something or other—usually described in French, which few could pronounce and fewer understand—the proverbial "Ah, Sweet Mystery of Life" was always feelingly rendered by so-or-so, on one occasion being reported in the local paper as "Ah, Sweet Misery of Life", the reception was a dream of loveliness down to the minutest detail—and on and on.

The wording of the wedding account has changed somewhat, but the traditional church wedding has not, nor have peoples' great interest and satisfaction in such a wedding. The bride is a shred when it is all over but, no matter, parents and friends had a beautiful time doing her in.

A young out-of-state boy—we'll call him LeRoy Mack—was apprehended in Camden, driving a stolen car. Having no folks to bail him out of jail, or to prevent his being locked up in the first place, he was forced to spend a few months behind bars, awaiting trial.

Keeping a white boy in jail was something new to Camden, and the women began feeling sorry for the young prisoner and began sending him food, games, and magazines. The men of the Methodist church decided to pitch in and be good Samaritans, feeling sure that the boy—good manners, that all-American look—was only an unfortunate kid who needed a helping hand to set him on the right road.

They bought him a suit of clothes and got the sheriff to release him in their custody during the daytime. On Sunday they took him to church and youth programs, and on week-days they took him home with them to do small chores. As the news spread, everyone in town wanted to get in a kindness lick. Those who could find easy jobs had the boy come and work a little, earn a little money, and eat all he could hold of their very best cooking.

Everywhere people were saying, "What a pity! What a nice kid!"

The jury could do no other than to find him guilty, but the judge, caught up in the sympathy swirl, gave the boy a year's suspended sentence, with kindly advice to "go home and behave yourself." Friends and well-wishers passed the hat, bought him a ticket, and gave him getting-home money. After putting him on the bus with pats on the back and "Good luck, God-bless-you" farewells, they went home feeling warm and happy, marveling at the miracle of redemption their good deeds had wrought.

A few days later they read in their morning papers that a LeRoy Mack, their befriended boy, had been jailed in Missis-sippi for stealing another car.

Interestingly enough, Camden people did a repeat of this same act, with variations, a few years later, with similar results. But, I have no doubt, if the occasion arose, they'd do it again. And I'd help.

People in Camden, white and black, are generous to a fault. Maybe one reason is that they have so many things to share. Share them they do. The men who hunt and fish share their trout, quail, doves, turkey, and venison with those who do not or cannot. Farmers share their farm machinery, their hired help, and farm produce; garden growers spend more time gathering vegetables and delivering them to friends than it takes to grow them; women take products of their culinary expertise everywhere they visit, like calling cards; flower en-thusiasts outshine each other, arranging and carrying flowers all over the place—sadness flowers, happiness flowers. Enter-taining without the presence of fresh garden flowers would be as much amiss to most Camden hostesses as going to church barefooted. Some share their concern by telephoning, others write letters. Some just pray, which may be the best of all. So many of the pleasant things of life go on that people hardly have time to kiss their spouses or wipe their children's noses. But it is a happy way, if one can survive.

On occasion sick people have to be readmitted to the hospital to be protected from visitors who apparently can't be denied admittance to the sick room. Even closed doors with "No Visitor" signs fail to stop them. As one crepe-hanger remarked, "It does a body good for him to know that there are other folks worse off."

But if the sick are well-wished to death, a person can't imagine, except vicariously, of course, the outpouring of concern and attention at the time of one's demise. Besides family and friends, people you scarcely knew or heard of will come by to pay their respects and bring cakes and pies for the multitude of kin who will come from far and near for the final rites. And never discount the food. It does help out. People do have to be fed, even at funerals, and the ingathering of the clan affords a fine opportunity to reminisce over food on anything but a gloomy note. Unless requested otherwise, enough flowers will descend on the bereaved household to stock a florist, the church will so overflow with people that the men will have to remain outside so the women can be seated.

Political office-holders are prominently present at all funerals within their jurisdiction, and if the deceased was himself a politician, the number of office-seeking politicians paying their respect is multiplied. The men outside usually have such a pow-wow, swapping yarns and talking politics, that the preacher may have to send word out for them to pipe down so he can get on with the service.

Once the service does get under way, you can count on the preacher giving you such a good send-off that St. Peter would find it difficult to turn you down. Unless forbidden by the family to do so, he may preach a "take-heed-lest" sermon to his captive audience. Only once, perhaps, did Camden people witness a funeral where the preacher expressed doubt of the deceased's being bound for a heavenly home. This rudeness, however, was inflicted on astonished friends and a hopping mad family by a backwoods preacher of little brain, who didn't know that even a man of the cloth had no business telling the unvarnished truth every time, much less at a graveside.

When death visits our little town, each one left knows that he is diminished, by little or much. No man here is a nobody. Everybody is a somebody. And the sadness at death is genuine. What is more, long memories hold the departed in mind and heart. The vacant church pew, the missing face, the voice, the laughter—the good and not-so-good are remembered and missed.

Strangely, and yet not so strange of mortal man, the cantankerous and cranky ones are remembered most clearly and most often recalled to mind. This should give some of us a certain satisfaction, except that each of us is just cranky enough to believe that he is the "regular" guy.

EIGHTEEN

Law and Disorder

Through the years following the Civil War, the South worked so hard to survive, and the North worked so hard building railroads and factories and getting rich, that not much notice was taken of minority groups. Those from the old country made do on whatever their wits could earn, clawing their way out of poverty and up the social ladder by determination and true grit.

The blacks, however, at least in the South, largely marked time in their depressed and deprived state until the 1930s. Then their discontent became a flickering flame of anger, which grew slowly at first but soon began to spread like a prairie fire. It was destined to endure longer than most of us would live, and it would require more active attention than well-meaning people and old-line politicians could imagine.

At about the same time, the social conscience of white Americans began to wake up and examine this new phenomenon, and the more they looked, the more concerned they became. Some decided that they should do what they could to dampen this blaze, even smother it. Others joined hands with the black leaders in an effort to eradicate the causes of the trouble, root and branch. Consequently, the latter set about not only to right old wrongs but also to rearrange patterns of thought and behavior and nail these changes to the wall with the hammer of the law. It was then that Act Two of the great racial drama began.

It is only fair that I designate the position from which I watched this struggle, thereby admitting that I could not know the thinking, feelings, actions, and reactions of all concerned. I wish also to state that in my observations I do not refer to all Black Belt whites or all Black Belt blacks. During these dramatic events I was largely isolated from the black community. I did not attend their mass meetings; I did not see the literature of the civil-rights workers or know what they and the local blacks talked about. And the blacks with whom I came in contact talked either very guardedly or not at all about what they were thinking or doing about what became a full-scale revolution.

History has already put this revolution into proper perspective on a larger scale, and whites in the Black Belt are gradually but surely doing so, here where some of the earliest scenes were acted out and where the stage was set for much of what happened elsewhere. But while history is in the making, it is not easy to see it evenly and fairly from both sides.

Many of the things whites heard during these days of trial were rumors, and often ugly ones at that. Some proved to be true, some had only a kernel of truth in them, and some were utterly false. It was very difficult at the time to sort them out. But because rumor, like propaganda, is such a powerful provoker of passions, it was one of the whites' earliest and most effective weapons to be used in defense of themselves throughout the conflict.

The first rumbles of thunder preceding the civil-rights movement came to the whites of the Black Belt in the early fifties from our nearby cities. There it was rumored that black women were joining together in Eleanor Clubs, so named for that indomitable power behind her husband, Franklin Delano Roosevelt. And the clubs were rightly so named, for Eleanor Roosevelt had sparked black freedom by fraternizing with people of all colors in and out of the White House and by championing civil rights, equal rights, and everybody's rights all over the place, even resigning from the Daughters of the American Revolution after they refused to allow Marian Anderson to sing in Constitution Hall.

As our southern whites understood it, these Eleanor Clubs were putting "uppity" notions into the heads of servants: cooks were to waste food and break dishes; Negro maids were to use their mistresses' toilet articles, to sweep dirt under rugs and down vents, and to quit cold if the word *nigger* was heard in the household. Also they were asking to be called Miss Thomas or Mrs. Jones instead of plain Annie or Ada.

Another rumor was heard about "Bumpers' Clubs." Their members were to shoulder whites off the streets, to push into the front of lines and prevent white women from "going first" through doors, or to send them whirling through revolving doors. Besides bumping, they were to try on all the finery in the ladies' wearing apparel departments just for the heck of it, and use dressing rooms and toilet facilities reserved for whites.

Negro men were said to be getting out of hand as well: black taxi drivers passing up whites, red caps refusing to take whites' luggage, waiters and bell-hops refusing service to anyone calling them "Boy" or "Uncle," and tips being refused if not sufficient, with service given according to the generosity of the tip.

Some of these reports had some truth in them. Many city cooks were refusing to clean house, housemaids were refusing to wash dishes or iron clothes, and nurses were refusing to do anything but mind the baby. Blacks were showing up in eating places and movie houses; black mothers with babies, bags, boxes, diapers, and bottles were riding Pullmans and day coaches; and if whites wanted to remain segregated, they had to travel in their own cars or stay at home.

The entrance of blacks into hitherto private domains of whites gave whites in the Black Belt plenty to talk about but little real concern until April 1954, when a bump of thunder shook them out of their complacency and made them realize that this integration business was not a way-off something or a somewhere-else thing, but a here-and-now thing. The Supreme Court on May 17, 1954, in the *Brown v. Board of Education of Topeka* case ruled that segregation in public schools violated the "equal protection" clause of the Fourteenth Amendment. A year later it declared that desegregation of public schools must proceed with "deliberate speed." Wherever white people got together, one could be fairly certain that the talk was about this shocking ruling and how it could be evaded, avoided, or nullified. The very idea of white children going to school with black children, playing together, growing up together, dancing together, and inevitably marrying each other! Never, never, never!

How might the decree be obeyed? The question was perhaps asked behind closed doors, but not out in public. After all, no white wanted to be called "nigger lover" or have a cross burned in his front yard.

There was even talk among a few whites of again seceding from the Union, but it was shadow talk and everybody knew it. Blacks, no doubt, talked about this miracle that had happened on their behalf, and I feel sure that they too had their shadow talk, but it was probably mixed with a solid determination.

As time swung along, because of every legal roadblock known to man being flung in its path, desegregation of schools failed to come about, and Black Belters began to feel that their politicians had been right when they promised "segregation forever." Consequently, they pushed this pot of stew onto the backburner of their minds, momentarily, to consider other compelling matters.

The very heavens seemed to be conspiring against the white

folks, for in the following year a young black preacher from, of all places, the "Cradle of the Confederacy" launched a crusade for freedom for his people that was to turn the South upside down and bring upon himself esteem and adoration from most blacks and scorn and hate from most southern whites. In 1955 Martin Luther King assumed the leadership of a bus boycott in Montgomery, Alabama, which won for his race the right to unsegregated seating in public carriers. From that time onward, many blacks hailed him as their Messiah, even as many Deep South whites called him the Anti-Christ.

Notwithstanding these and other disturbances, until the sixties, most Black Belt whites still boasted that "their" Negroes were as contented and as faithful as they had always been. "It just can't happen here," was what was said about trouble abroad, or "It won't happen here." A favorite warning was: "Never let the Negro get his toe in the door, for if he does, he'll take over."

But the toe was already in the door, and a wind was assisting it with pressure that grew stronger by the hour. It was most obvious that blacks were moving up in the world. More and more of them were driving cars! For Southern whites, first seeing blacks driving their own cars was like first seeing them on television: it surprised some whites, shocked some, and irritated others. In the Deep South, driving cars and appearing on television had long been reserved for whites; now whites declared that Negroes on TV were too-too clever or too-too sweet and entirely too familiar with whites. Whites could turn off their television when blacks appeared, but they couldn't turn off the cars. They swore that Negroes were hogging the road and driving like crazy, and maybe some were. Having this new power at their fingertips—this new right to make whites wait for them, to obey their signals, and to give them half the road—had to be heady stuff for some blacks.

But automobile dealers had discovered a bonanza in the market for used cars; many wheezing their last gasp when sold and soon to be abandoned in a ditch or backyard. Roadsides became dotted with these smoke-spewing rattle traps, jacked up, hoods lifted, radiators belching steam, while their occupants patiently awaited help from somewhere to get them on to their destinations. But drive these carcasses Negroes did, loaded down with family or friends, so long as the wheels turned and they had a thin dime for gas. And who could blame them for starving a little in order to ride in style after having had only mules and wagons or "foots" for transportation for so long?

Hand-operated washing machines began to appear on sagging front porches and aerials began sprouting from every cabin roof. TV had come into the blacks' homes, and they could now, to their greater enlightenment and greater discontent with their own plight, experience the whole wide world beyond. White people approved of ownership of these washing machines as common sense, but most deplored the extravagance of owning a television set while still using a privy for a toilet. (Personally, I considered the blacks' choice exceedingly wise.) But for these gadgets, sold to them for a little down and a little a week, including exorbitant interest, they paid several times' value received; and often an appliance would be reclaimed by the salesman if a payment was missed or a day overdue.

What really disturbed the white folks, however, were the suspicious visitors from outside, riding the roads and roaming the back country by day and by night: Freedom Riders, civil-rights workers, NAACPers, organizers of whatever kind. Surely, most of us thought, whatever they were doing or saying boded no good for white folks. Consequently, trespass signs went up on some property, gates were locked, tenants were warned, and some were "put in the road." A few of these strangers were arrested on various charges, but on and on they came. Small, clandestine meetings grew bigger and bolder until mass meetings held in the black churches became commonplace. But black participants went quietly about their regular jobs exactly as if nothing unusual were going on.

The Ku Klux Klan, trying to resurrect bones of the long-dead Confederacy, shook out their sheets, held meetings, made speeches, and burned a Negro church here and there; while many whites who couldn't stomach the Klan joined the local White Citizens' Council, hoping through the power of press and politics to maintain the status quo.

By the late fifties ominous clouds were clotting all over the South. The very air smelled of storm. President Dwight Eisenhower sent the National Guard to Little Rock in September 1957, and President John Kennedy sent federal marshals in 1962 to the University of Mississippi, after a federal court had ordered the admittance of a black student, James Meredith, to Ole Miss. In 1963 Martin Luther King clashed with "Bull" Conner, the chief of police of Birmingham, where, after marches to force integration, a church was bombed and four black children were killed. In the same year, Governor George Wallace, pretending to make good his "segregation forever" oath to the white people of Alabama, stood in the "school house door" of The University of Alabama, only to accept defeat instead of victory when two black students were admitted. No matter the lost causes; the southern politicians continued to damn the Supreme Court and the Feds, and their supporters continued to sic them on to champion their beleaguered cause.

At last, in the spring of 1965, the storm broke in all its fury in the adjoining county of Dallas, in the friendly, genteel little city of Selma, of all places. Dr. King had chosen his ground carefully when he attempted to force voter registration of Negroes here; Selma was deep South, Black Belt, entirely segregated with but few Negro voters, and all in Wallace's front yard. It would be an eyeball-to-eyeball confrontation between the civil-rights leader and the governor.

After fruitless weeks of haranguing between Negroes and whites, mass meetings, boycotts, sit-ins, unlicensed marches and demonstrations, skirmishes with police, subsequent arrests, the air filled with charges and countercharges of misconduct, a march from Selma to Montgomery was scheduled by King, no doubt to dramatize, on a massive scale, the cause for which all the prior pressures had been applied.

What followed turned into a tragedy of the worst kind for the whites and a victory of tremendous proportions for the blacks. Wallace at first denied permission for the march, throwing down the gauntlet, as it were, when granting permission might have thwarted or defused the venture. King defied the order to desist, and what followed was the confrontation at Pettus Bridge.

Watching television that morning, I witnessed the clash. The use of horses and billy clubs by police turned what might have been a mere incident into a tragedy of a whole new dimension. My heart turned to lead. In a vague sort of way I knew what that picture, turned on all over the world, would do to the South, the white South, to us here in the Black Belt. It was a time to weep. And I am sure there were many who, along with me, did just that.

By the time Judge Frank M. Johnson, Jr. gave his order that the march be permitted, hundreds of newsmen were on hand, hundreds of cameras, thousands of persons sympathetic to the civil-rights cause, both black and white. The march was made, but during it the Rev. James Reeb and Mrs. Viola Liuzzo were murdered by whites, who thereby heaped the ultimate shame upon us.

Martin Luther King had won an unprecedented victory for his people and the adulation of the world beyond the Southland. Our Southern whites had lost the first campaign in a war that was lost before it was begun; we had won only sadness for ourselves and ill-will from abroad. The fact that this was a mild incident compared to what was to happen elsewhere later on was no help in lessening the anger heaped upon our heads.

In an attempt to understand why such a calamity had been allowed to happen, I asked myself some questions. Who was to blame? Was it Martin Luther King? George Wallace? Frank Johnson? Was it the officers who were obeying orders? Was it Selma? The South? Did it just happen as a quirk of fate, or were the causes rooted in days long past? Could it have been that old specter of Reconstruction days, the white man's fear of the power of the Negro vote?

Perhaps it would be fair to say that no one thing was wholly to blame. Time, custom, and circumstance had converged into a single beam, passed through the powerful lens of public opinion, and finally focused on highly flammable material. Combustion was inevitable.

The curtain had come down on Act Two of the Black Belt's racial drama, but it left the larger part of the audience angry indeed.

Stones were cast, at Selma and at Alabama, and because we were a part of it, at the South. And because we stood against world opinion, the stones hurt. We cast our little pebbles in defense or defiance, but they carried no farther than our own boundaries. Selma and Montgomery became the Sodom and Gomorrah of the South. Tourists went hundreds of miles out of their way to avoid passing through our state, for fear of being murdered. Alabamians visiting other areas had fists shaken in their faces, bricks thrown through car windows, and tires slashed. Many, being denied maid and redcap service because they were from Alabama, removed all tell-tale evidence from their luggage and even attempted to disguise their southern speech to avoid mistreatment.

In Congress, the first cake off this sizzling griddle was a new civil-rights bill in 1965, which suspended literacy tests in those states and counties in which less than 50 percent of the voter-age population was registered at the time of the presidential election of 1964, applying specifically (though not exclusively) to the Deep South states with heavy Negro populations who had been denied the vote. In addition, the bill provided that federal examiners could enroll voters in places where discriminatory practices had been employed. *De facto* segregation was allowed elsewhere while *de jure* segregation, common to the South, was outlawed. Subsequently, federal observers were sent into all Black Belt polling places where blacks outnumbered whites.

Once voter restrictions were lifted, civil-rights workers returned to Wilcox County, as to other Black Belt counties, to see that all blacks of voting age were registered. At first, whites said among themselves that the blacks wouldn't bother to register. They were wrong. The blacks came, they stood for hours in sun, wind, and cold, and they continued to come until every name was on the voting list.

It is true that during these trying times some things were done by some whites that were deplorable and ugly; but so far as I know, they were acts committed by angry citizens and not by officers of the law. Some civil-rights workers were threatened and advised to leave town; some so-called "meddling" preachers were beaten up, anyone using a camera was apt to have it smashed, and a few innocents suffered abuse as victims of mistaken identity. These regrettable incidents not only grieved most Camden whites, but they also shot holes into the rather proud assumption by whites that their friendliness and hospitality were unparalleled in this land of ours.

NINETEEN

End of the Tunnel

When Dr. Martin Luther King came to Camden in February 1965 Sheriff Lummie Jenkins met him with a friendly salute, "Hi, Preacher!" He invited King into his office, where they chatted amicably about various things.

"I understand," said Dr. King, "that a person can't vote in Wilcox County unless he has a qualified voter to vouch for him."

"That's right," said Lummie.

"Well, how about you acting as voucher for these newly registered voters around here?"

"I'm not allowed," Lummie informed him. "A voucher can't hold a political office."

"Mind if I look around town for vouchers?" asked King.

"Inquire around," Lummie answered, knowing full well that all voters in Wilcox were white, and not a one would be caught dead vouching for a Negro.

Lummie told Dr. King that race relations had been exceptionally good until recent disturbances by outside agitators; that his department performed, almost daily, acts of aid or mercy for blacks in danger or distress, and that he saw to many emergencies out of his own pocket.

Dr. King knew this; he had been told by the blacks themselves. "My people speak well of you," King said.

King wanted to know why the blacks had to register at the old, considerably run-down jail. Lummie assured him that if it was good enough for whites, it ought to be good enough for blacks. King reminded Lummie that there were six thousand possible black voters in the county, and if they were registered and vouched for, they just might elect a Negro sheriff. "Many of them tell me," Lummie laughed, "that they don't want one of their own 'ruling' over them."

"Maybe," said King. "We'll see."

On leaving, Dr. King asked where he might find a restaurant. Lummie pointed across the street, but a "closed" sign was already hung on the door. "Try the back street," Lummie suggested. "They'll be tickled pink to have you."

And it is a wonder that a sign doesn't hang in that little back-street cafe saying "Martin Luther King ate here," for he did eat there more than once.

Black and white civil-rights workers, largely young people of both sexes, used a Negro church on the outskirts of town not only for a headquarters and rallying place for marches, but also for living quarters as well. This latter arrangement was particularly annoying to many whites, as it must have been to many Negroes. Whites were shocked to see young black-white couples walking the streets of Camden, holding hands or with arms about each other, often the girl's head on her companion's shoulder. There was much muttering and head-shaking about this, but when these young people indulged in petting on the benches in front of the courthouse, they went too far. At this sight, even the children gawked and pointed in astonishment, and mamas herded them home as quickly as possible.

It was then that Lummie quietly got paint and brush and had a trusty paint the benches and put up "wet paint" signs. As soon as the benches dried, he had them painted again, until this particular problem disappeared.

Inside the courthouse, one black girl, bolder than the rest, decided to integrate the drinking fountains. "I'm tired of drinking this colored water," she announced. "Think I'll try the white water and see how it tastes." And so she did. When a group of her friends came in to follow up her victory, the water had been cut off. Both fountains were later removed, and people said, quite truthfully, that Wilcox's courthouse was the driest in the state of Alabama.

It is told that during those days Lummie had a delegation of several strange blacks come to him, requesting that he protect them when they attempted to integrate one of the two white restaurants in Camden. Lummie said he was too busy, and this was not properly his business anyway. As the group started to leave, Lummie suggested that they give him their home addresses. The spokesman of the group wanted to know why.

"I'd just like to know where to send your remains," Lummie said.

"Remains?" they wondered if they had heard correctly.

"Yes," Lummie told them. "It'll just save me a lot of trouble later."

"But," asked one, his enthusiasm somewhat subdued, "do you really think the owner of that place might shoot us?"

"I don't think anything about it," Lummie assured them. "I know damn' well he will."

The integrators talked it over and decided to find another target for their efforts.

Most of the demonstrators in the Camden marches were school children, who were said to have been enticed into playing hooky by "outside agitators." Many of them probably did not know why they were demonstrating, but they had a lot of fun after they were stopped before reaching the courthouse; they sang, clapped hands, and made faces and stuck out tongues at passing whites. Under ordinary circumstances, these moppets, whether black or white, would have had their backsides blistered by their own parents for their impudence.

During these days, as I walked past a bus filled with black children, one little girl stuck her head out the window and called to me, "We're gonna bury you, we're gonna bury you!" I laughed then, and I still do, at a remark that a short time before would have been unthinkable. But in later days during the violence that engulfed our land, I came to wonder if whites and blacks were going to bury each other before peace prevailed.

There was one march that might easily have ended in real trouble. Word had gone out that outside agitators were in town, and permission had been given for a march that would be climaxed with speeches on the courthouse lawn. Women and children were advised to stay at home, and most of them did, but by midmorning, Camden began filling up with men, coming in from all over the county, and some from farther away.

Nearly every white man in the county owns a pickup truck, and nearly every truck is equipped with a double or triple gunrack, hung behind the seat. These racks aren't there for looks. They are there for guns, and guns are there. That day, as someone observed, there were enough pickups in Camden with enough shotguns in them to start a small war.

The sheriff and mayor spent hours before the march talking to these and other onlookers, white and black, earnestly requesting them to keep calm and, more important, asking them to help keep the peace by alerting the law to anything that looked suspicious. The march went off peaceably, even though the black speaker accused white men of fighting integration by day and practicing it by night, further declaring that someday blacks would take over the courthouse and rule the county. Such a speech might have been countered by violence, had not the whites present, having been made to feel it a duty to keep order, begun by keeping it themselves.

The culmination of all these dangerous days, when whites were seeing their cherished traditions violated, was the primary election of 1966. In accordance with the provisions of the Voting Rights Act of 1965, observers were dispatched to the Black Belt to observe voting practices. Law-enforcement men came from all over the country, and they came expecting trouble. They admitted, after tensions relaxed, that they had been briefed by lecture and study on how to carry on under riot conditions.

Election officials and watchers in the polling booths took great pains to be kind and gracious to these strangers, and they took even greater pains to help the old, infirm, and illiterate blacks to vote. Local restaurants sent hot dinners for the poll workers, and everyone became so chummy before the day was over that the observers expressed a desire to come back and stay longer.

At one crossroad booth, however, one observer did get a fright. When a truck driving by repeatedly backfired, the observer thought he was being shot at and dived under the table. With considerable amusement the workers allowed him to believe for a time that his suspicions were correct.

After the voting was over, the town came alive with reporters from all over the country. Even John Doar, assistant to Attorney General Katzenbach, was here. The next day Doar said on national television that the election had "gone off with comfort and ease." One reporter, emerging from the phone booth on the courthouse lawn, was exasperated with his New York paper. "They won't believe a word I tell them," he said. "And it wouldn't surprise me if they print just the opposite."

A reporter from the *Manchester Guardian,* who lived in Salisbury, Rhodesia, smiled with understanding of our Southern predicament and promised to give us a good press. Another from a Chicago paper said he had covered the Selma march and had not only come to like Selma and Alabama, but since then had visited Selma with his family. In light of later developments he had written a public apology on his own behalf and that of his paper, for condemning us so caustically in the early days of the civil-rights ordeal.

Contrary to expectations, Camden's blacks did not vote in a bloc. Lummie Jenkins was reelected sheriff by a combination of white and black votes, and Camden's whites breathed a sigh of relief. Things had not been so bad as we or the federal observers had expected. In fact, it was a banner day for peace and tranquility.

However, there were many sad consequences in the wake of these days and years of strife. Public parks, playgrounds, and swimming pools were closed; libraries took out their reading tables; rural movie houses closed in favor of drive-ins. Stools and seats were ripped up in neighborhood drugstores, and these old rendezvous for sweethearts or for old folks with tired feet, or for hungry kids wanting a banana split or a chocolate sundae, all disappeared from the downtown streets of Black Belt towns.

Most unfortunate of all, the disorders left a residue of ill-will and distrust between the races. Many white men, and black as well, pocketed pistols, and white women began carrying weapons in their handbags or in the pockets of their cars. People began locking their cars and their homes when they left them. Churches argued and split over racial matters and over how to disburse their money. Conservative whites were set against liberal whites, militant blacks against moderate blacks. Whatever slender lines of communication had existed between the races were temporarily severed.

But only temporarily. In a few short years tensions have relaxed and "back to normal" is the mood. But there is a difference. Black and white lives are touching in new places, in business, government, and public services, and quietly but surely forging a new relation between races. In the last election Martin Luther King's prediction became a fact: a black was elected sheriff of our county. On his shoulders lies a heavy burden of proving to whites that his office will be administered efficiently and even-handedly to both races, and an equally heavy burden will lie on the shoulders of whites to accept in good faith and with goodwill the first black elected to a place of authority in Wilcox County since Reconstruction days.

This is no time to look back. The bridges are burned behind

us. We either travel the low road as adversaries, or we become yoke-fellows and travel the high road together.

TWENTY

Our Beloved Physician

It was Monday morning in the early forties. The small white waiting room of Dr. J. Paul Jones, affectionately known as Dr. Paul, was crowded with an accumulation of aches and pains, as was the Negro waiting room, adjoining but separate.

"Bad as one o' these city offices," grumbled a turkey-necked, corrugated-faced farmer to his companion in the next chair. "You wait all day suffering and nigh 'bout dying befo' you git a squint o' the doctor." He continued to clack his loose-fitting false teeth between audible sighs and grunts which were probably born of irritation rather than pain.

"And when they git ahold ter you," the other oldster shouted back at him, as if he were deaf, "they're so durn close-mouthed, they won't tell you what ails you to save their souls, ner what they're doctoring you with."

"Fact is," the first continued, squirming in his seat, "half the time they're jes projecking with a body, slicing you open befo' you can bat an eye and punching you full o' holes with needles. I'd rather be shot by a cannon any day."

"Twouldn't be so bad," his companion sympathized, "if they won't in such a dad-blamed hurry that they can't set down and pass the time o' day with you. No, sirree, they ain't got time to say pea-turkey. 'N they don't see you face to face long enough to recognize you in yo' clothes. They git you in there and strip you naked befo' they lay eyes on you."

The old fellow's grumpiness shattered as his own wisecrack tickled him into laughing.

There was some truth and a lot of genuine regret, shared by all of us, in what the oldster was saying. At the turn of the century there were thirty-five doctors in Wilcox County, more than in Birmingham's (now) populous county of Jefferson, or in Mobile or Montgomery counties. As the saying went, there was a doctor on every hill, and when one was sent for, he came a hopping, as fast as old dobbin could bring him by buggy or in saddle, and he stayed all day or night, or all week, if need be. And he charged so little that few people made the effort to go to his office.

However, in the forties there were only four active physicians in Wilcox County, all over fifty, for more than twenty-six thousand people scattered over nearly a thousand square miles; and instead of practicing out of saddlebags, from which they dispensed calomel, quinine, paregoric, morphine, digitalis, fever medicine, and cough syrup, they preferred to test and diagnose in their offices where it could be more properly done.

These doctors were still having a rough time financially. Though money was a bit more plentiful than during the Great Depression, most Negroes were still paying their doctors with a bumble-footed rooster, a gallon of sorghum syrup, or a peck of sweet potatoes. And most whites were paying their bills once a year, in the fall after harvest. That is, if there was anything left after the bank and the boll weevil got through with them. As Doctor Paul remarked, "During those years we couldn't get down to root causes of problems. We just did the best we could, by guess and by God. And if we knew the root causes, we couldn't eliminate them, not nearly always, for lack of facilities at home and no means or money to send a patient forty miles away to a hospital."

After looking me over, a stiff-starched, egg-shaped woman squeezed into the old sofa beside me and wanted to know what ailed me. No sooner had I happily begun to enumerate my rare and peculiar symptoms than I was deluged with enthusiastic accounts of her own, so much more distressful that I could no longer take pride in mine. The whole room soon broke into such animated chatter about carbuncles, snake bite, fits, and birthing babies, that when a name was called, the patient rose reluctantly, as a bear pried from a honey pot. The truth may be that the waiting room was taking over part of yesterday's doctor's job, patients acting as a sort of wailing wall for each other where they just might talk their troubles to death.

My turn came at last. At that time I had lived in Camden only a few years, but it was quite evident that among the people I knew, Doctor Paul was the most loved and respected person in Camden. Already my love and admiration for him were sure, and they were to grow through the years.

"Howdy, Sister," he greeted me, sighing ponderously with fatigue. In later years, when I had achieved the privilege, it would be "Howdy, Grandma."

No wonder he was weary and gray-haired at fifty, with so many people to care for and so many living in the hills, swamps, and cotton patches where he had to travel daily and nightly to attend births, deaths, serious illnesses, and, sometimes and most frustrating of all, a person who was not really ill but, just the same, thought he was dying—always in the middle of the night. And on Saturday nights, up all hours sewing up slashes and setting bashed bones.

When he had turned me over to his nurse, Mrs. Huckabee, for tests of various sorts, I had time to recall some of the bizarre stories I had already heard, often from Doctor Paul himself, which were commonplace in his practice. And as the years passed, more would be added.

There was old Sim Carson from across the Alabama River, who burst into the doctor's office one morning as wild as a loco steer, two men holding him to restrain him from violence.

"Save me, Doctor, save me!" he was screaming. "I'm gone plum crazy, Doctor. Or else I'm dying right now."

Doctor Paul took him by the shoulder. "Hush that fuss, damn it, and tell me what ails you, Sim," he demanded in a tone of voice that required a sensible response.

"Lord, Lord," Sim calmed down enough to say, "I got screw worms on the brain."

"Screw worms?" the doctor repeated incredulously, pushing Sim into a chair and getting a hypo ready to quiet him.

"Well, you're screwy, all right. Who ever heard of anybody having screw worms?"

"Boss, I sho ain't never heard o' it, but they're there. I been sneezing an' blowin' 'em out. I tell you the God's truth, they're eatin' me up."

At that time the screw fly was a menance to live-stock, particularly cattle. The female lays her eggs in cuts, sores, or abrasions, the eggs hatch quickly into masses of small white grubs, developing rapidly into adult flies. Because they live on live tissue, unless removed or destroyed, they will, in time, attack some vital organ and kill their host. Actually there was no reason why they shouldn't attack a human being except that people are able to protect themselves from them.

Doctor Paul examined Sim's nasal passages and, sure enough, Sim was right. His nose was full of grubs. No wonder he was nearly crazy, for they had already eaten a hole through the cartilaginous membrane between the nasal passages.

"Don't let me die, Doctor," Sim kept repeating. "Charge me anything in God's world, n' I'll pay you if it takes the rest o' time."

"Shut up," Doctor Paul told him. "You know you never paid a doctor's bill in your life."

In flushing out Sim's nose, Doctor Paul counted thirty grubs, but a few resisted or were beyond the reach of liquid or forceps. A cotton pack saturated with chloroform brought out five more, but there was one more in sight which refused to be dislodged. After the effects of the choloform wore off and Sim came to, he suddenly sneezed and out came that last one. Such a happy person rarely existed as Sim.

"Now that you can talk sense," said Doctor Paul, "tell me how the devil you got those blamed things in your nose?"

"It was this way," Sim explained. "I had a tooth pulled, n' the thing hurt so bad til I took a big swig o' licker 'n went sound to sleep on the porch floor. While I was sleep the fly musta gone up my nose and laid her eggs."

"Well, I guess you'll stay sober awhile now," Doctor Paul told him.

"But, Doctor," Sim began, remembering all he had volunteered about charging him just anything, "you remember that I'm a po' creeter with a house full o' chillun . . ."

"'N you haven't got any money to pay the doctor," Doctor Paul finished. "You get out of here, you rascal. I'll charge you what I please, and you better pay it, or next time I'll let the screw worms eat you up alive."

Sim's predicament was somewhat similar to that of Isom's. Having been to Doctor Paul with a head injury, which was duly disinfected and bandaged, Isom was instructed to return in two days for a fresh dressing. But because he felt no pain, Isom neglected to return until something curious began to happen. As he explained it, "The bandage got to wiggling and working like it was alive."

Doctor Paul opened the bandage, now ten days old, and found what he expected, a head full of maggots, working like only the devilish little scavengers could work. "Well, I'll be damned," he exploded, "the worms aren't waiting for you to die, Isom, they've got a head start on you already."

However, after Isom's head was ridded of its busy inhabitants, his wound was found to be as clean as a hound's tooth. The maggots had done a good job of cleaning out the putrid flesh, and Isom was well on his way to recovery. He didn't wait ten days before coming in for a fresh dressing.

One day a child was brought into the office in the throes of a convulsion. While receiving attention, the child vomited up a mass of roundworms, some as long as pencils, which took out across the floor in all directions. Mrs. Huckabee, having a phobia for crawling creatures, dropped her tray of nurse's paraphernalia and, screaming, fled the place.

This child died. Doctor Paul said that it was not unusual for people having violent abdominal pain to be sent to hospitals as surgery cases and found to have knots of roundworms in the stomach and intestines. Gotten through filth from eating dirt or eating from unclean food vessels, roundworms were once a cause of many deaths among rural children. And, he added, their infestation is still much more widespread than is imagined. Fortunately, by midcentury, hookworm had been largely eradicated.

There was another less gruesome case of worms. Matt Davy came in, all atremble, eyes wild, declaring he had a snake inside him. "You're crazy as a betsy-bug. Or drunk as a monkey," Doctor Paul told him.

"Naw, sir," Matt declared, "he sticks his head up back in my throat when I open my mouth."

"Well, open up," Doctor Paul told him, "and let's see this pet of yours."

Matt opened up. Doctor Paul shined his flashlight inside and, sure enough, a tremendous worm was poking his head up back in Matt's throat. "Damn," Doctor Paul swore, "if I didn't pull out a twelve-inch worm." Matt was promptly treated and as promptly cured.

Doctor Paul discovered he had a serious problem with the timidity of his Negro patients when he tried to find out what symptoms he had to work with. Whenever he asked, "Have you ever had so or so?" the answer would be "yes-suh," or if he asked, "Do you have a pain in the stomach or chest?" it was the same. If he asked the question this way, "You haven't got swimming in the head, have you?" the answer would be "No-suh," and always the same with negatively put questions. Finally, he had his black nurse question his black patients first. They were apt to tell her the real truth.

Doctor Paul heard that the blacks were saying among themselves that "When Doctor Paul look at you and shake his head and don't say nothing, you're a dead nigger." Consequently, he had to be careful not to shake his head at anyone in his care.

Many were the times when Doctor Paul was called out to deliver babies when the cases were too stubborn or complicated for the midwife. One such case occurred on a freezing cold night. After a ride down trails and over branches, he arrived at the patient's cabin. There being no hot water, he had the midwife, known as a granny, bring in a chunk of ice from the waterbucket on the porch and melt it on the hearth. While Doctor Paul was busy, the midwife "histed" her skirt to warm her seat, and a live coal popped out on her. Not waiting on ceremony she plopped down in the basin of precious water to put out the fire on her backside. "Then she got a blistering from me," Doctor Paul added. "It took half an hour to draw another bucket of water from the well and heat it."

One stormy night a man from across the river came on foot, seeking help for his wife, who had been a long time in labor. The river was up; no ferry was running. After rowing across in a skiff, the husband located the mule he had left tied to a tree. Doctor Paul mounted and the husband walked, leading the way in the darkness, the old mule stumbling through mud, the rain coming down in sheets. When they arrived, backwater was already seeping through the floor of the cabin. "We put the patient up on a table," Doctor Paul said. "The granny had given the mother up. It was a forceps case requiring chloroform. The granny was appointed anesthetist, holding the saturated cotton over the patient's nose and counting ten, release, count ten and release. Along the way, the counting trailed off; there was a clunking squish to the floor. The midwife had passed out. The husband was pressed into service, and the baby was delivered just as daylight began to sift through the cracks in the wall. "The rain had stopped falling," said Doctor Paul, "but it was midday before I got back to Camden."

"In several deliveries," Doctor Paul recalls, "there were no clothes for the newborn baby, and no clean articles I could lay hands on, so I wrapped the babies up in my shirt. I've delivered them by flashlight, by lamplight, even by burning pine knots."

It was not unusual for some people to misunderstand Doctor Paul's diagnosis. He once told an elderly man that he had bronchitis, but in fun he pronounced it "bronketis." When the secretary inquired what his trouble was, the patient answered that Doctor Paul said he had "brown skeeters." There was the woman who told her friends that Doctor Paul had diagnosed her husband's problem as an enlarged prostitute gland.

Another called him one day, saying that she wanted him to come see her husband. Asked what the trouble might be, she said. "Jeb, he ain't been to the johnny in a week, so I give him a red-devil pill and an enigma, but he ain't done nothing yet." "If you've done all that with no results, I guess he does need a doctor," Doctor Paul said.

There was a black woman who, on half a dozen Saturday nights, called the doctor to say that she was bad cut by her boy friend.

"But," said Doctor Paul, "it is the strangest thing, most couples who come in here after one has slashed or bashed the other, act like turtle doves before they leave, completely forgiven and reconciled."

On another occasion a man came in in great pain. It seemed probable from his symptoms that he had an intestinal obstruction. On examination it was discovered that it was an impaction of watermelon seed in the lower colon. As Doctor Paul said, "I dislodged enough watermelon seed to plant Wilcox County." And as his nurse later added, "Doctor Paul swore like a sailor, but nobody but a saint would do a job like that."

Just talking to the doctor often did a patient more good than his medicine. There was Aunt Sarah. She waddled into the office leaning heavily on her knobby walking stick.

"What ails you, Auntie?" Doctor Paul asked.

"I don't know, Doctor. I'm jus' sick."

"Hell, I know you're sick or you wouldn't be here. What hurts? You got a broke leg or fixing to have a baby?"

Fanning herself with her straw hat, Aunt Sarah chuckled. She understood Doctor Paul's gruff good humor, even when it might be evidence of frayed patience.

"Lord Jesus, Doctor, you know I been condemned nigh unto forty years."

"Maybe you call it condemned, but these young girls 'round here would call it a reprieve."

Aunt Sarah laughed shallowly, probably not understanding what the word "reprieve" meant. "You already tol' me I got the high blood," she said, "but whenever I washes I git the blind staggers."

"Well, haven't I told you to stay out of that washtub?"

"How I'm gonna stay clean, Doctor?"

"Take that walking stick of yours and frail the daylights out of half a dozen chillun and grandchillun of yours if they don't wait on you. It's time you sat down and shelled peas and pieced quilts."

"Yes-suh, you tol' me that already, too."

"I'm telling you again because I don't want to have to help bury you. By the way," he added, "what you doing with all those bandaids sticking all over you? Been in a cat fight?"

"No-suh, they're fer my rheumatics. Wherever I hurts I stick one on. 'N they're doing me all the good."

"Well, that's great," Doctor Paul smiled. "I better go out and get myself a bale of the things."

"You gonna give me some medicine, ain't you, Doctor?"

"You're darn tootin' I am. I'll fix you up so you'll be as frisky as a spring lamb."

Aunt Sarah left with a bottle of liniment, one of milk of magnesia, one of aspirin, and something for her "high blood." She was as happy as a child with a magic wand.

That Monday morning, Doctor Paul finally called me into his office. His diagnosis was more from his knowledge of me and my lifestyle than from test or chart. My fatigue, he told me, was probably caused by low blood pressure instead of laziness (as I feared); my headaches by tension (as I hoped) rather than a brain tumor; my nerves a product of pressure (as I suspected) rather than of creeping insanity.

"You need to slow down, relax, and stop doing so many unnecessary things," he said. "But I can't," I began. "You can if you want to," he countered. "You aren't indispensable, you know." Maybe I wasn't, but I definitely thought I was. I didn't argue, however. As I started to leave, I remarked, "Well, I'll try desperately hard to follow your advice."

"Wait right there," he said somewhat sternly. "There you go with 'try desperately hard'. Now young lady, get that word 'desperately' out of your vocabulary. That's your trouble, trying desperately hard to do everything."

For years now I have been reminded of that advice, and my efforts to rid my life of that word have been a battle, but the very fact that I have survived for so long may be attributed to the measure of success I achieved.

Until his death in December 1975, Doctor Paul Jones was still doctoring us. His devotion to his patients and dedication to his profession were matched only by his stamina and strength of character. Now we have a spic-and-span little hospital that bears his name, where doctoring is made easier; and health insurance, both public and private, helps us bear the burden of expense.

Doctor Paul admitted that he had to unlearn most of what he learned in those early years of practice and that he had to study, even while he ate, to keep up with new medicines and techniques. There are two younger doctors in Camden now, but for years Dr. Paul, with the county-health physician, Dr. E. L. McIntosh, bore the burden of healing in half the county when rural medicine was a killing profession—for the doctor.

In addition to his practice, Doctor Paul held a dozen important medical offices in county, state, and nation; he was president of both county and state medical associations, a member of the National Commission for Better Care of the Patient, of Rural Medical Services, of the State Board of Mental Health, and many more.

He worked faithfully through the years for more and better medical schools, more nursing programs and training aids, and for greater incentives for medical students to become general practitioners and to enter rural practice rather than specialized practice in urban areas. As a member of the Mental Health Board, he was particularly concerned with the varied and profound problems of modernizing our antiquated mental institutions.

Dr. Paul Jones was a somebody. Camden will always be proud of him. Both county and state honored him for his outstanding services, but the greatest tribute that can be paid him does not reside in plaques and citations; it is in the love and esteem in which he will always be held by his many friends, both black and white.

TWENTY-ONE

Under the Pecan Tree

One could not leave Camden without a visit under the pecan tree on the courthouse lawn, where the men, and men only, have the time to prognosticate, pontificate, and argue about everything under the sun. As Mister Frank Dexter, a wise old bachelor, once said, "A monumental amount of ignorance and speculation gets sworn to as absolute fact under that pecan tree."

Besides gossiping about all the hanky-panky going on, which men enjoy as much as women, and griping about free handouts to no-'count folks, high prices of stuff that ain't worth a continental, and the ruination of the country by all those darn crackpots in Washington, there is always a spate of stories. Usually a sort of character story where the life-long knowledge of the person concerned spices whatever is told about him.

Nothing pleases the pecan-tree sitters more than a joke on one of the courthouse crowd. While Judge McLeod was probate judge, a persistent salesman of pesticides and disinfectants, known as Little Hitt, called on the judge, attempting to sell him a sizable amount of his products for use in the courthouse and jail. The salesman's high-pressure style irritated the judge from the start; the more the little fellow insisted, the more annoyed the judge became and the more adamantly he refused. Finally, to get rid of his pest, he suggested that Hitt go over to the jail and see if Lummie Jenkins, the sheriff, needed anything.

Contrary to what the judge expected, Lummie felt that he could use a few gallons of the stuff in and around his ancient, decrepit jail. Not knowing that Judge McLeod had seen the salesman, Lummie went over to the judge's office, the salesman along with him.

The judge had his feet up on the desk, his chair swiveled so that he was turned away from the door when the two walked in. "Judge," Lummie began, "I'm getting some of Mister Hitt's disinfectant for the jail. Don't you want some over here?"

Without turning around Judge McLeod answered. "You get what you want, but I've already told that sawed-off sonofabitch that I don't want a thing he's got."

"Well," said Lummie, "you're telling him again, because he's right here with me."

The upshot of that blast was that Judge McLeod, evidently ashamed of what he had said, made what lame apologies he could, then bought a whole barrel of the salesman's product.

If Governor Meek Miller, known as the Sturdy Oak of Wilcox, with his watch chain looping across his ample waist, passed by the pecan tree, someone was sure to recall some of the stories about him.

Serving at the time as circuit judge, Meek Miller ran for and was later elected governor of Alabama in 1932 on a strong economy platform, one not only popular during those terrible Depression days, but also necessary for the salvation of the state's critical financial condition. People in Camden, his home, knew that his financial stance was not a pose but a sincere part of the governor's staunch character and frugal way of living. Hence when his name is mentioned, always with considerable pride, the stories told about him often concern his Spartan habits, stories enhanced by the knowledge that he was a man of considerable wealth.

His young nephew, James Miller, who acted as his chauffeur, recalls that while campaigning, "every night when the judge was ready to retire he would call me into his room for devotions. There in his slit-tail night shirt, Uncle Meek would read a passage of Scripture, say a prayer, and then for night-caps, serve us glasses of buttermilk."

Because of his fondness for home-churned buttermilk and butter, when he went to Montgomery as governor, he took his milch cow with him and had her duly installed on the mansion grounds.

After his election, the governor, deciding to combine business with a rest, made a trip to New York City. He and Feagan, his campaign director, went to the Pennsylvania Hotel, where the governor insisted on a four-dollars-a-day room. But the hotel was crowded, and the clerk put them in an eight-dollars-a-day room, charging them only four dollars for it. The governor was delighted with his plush quarters but only because, he said, "we're saving four-dollars-a-day on all this finery."

Again, during the governor's stay in Montgomery, his official car was his own, a Dodge of somewhat ancient vintage. His chauffeur, Will, was having quite a patching and pumping problem keeping the old limousine afloat. One day, completely fed up, he came to the governor complaining. "Governor," he said, "we've got to get a new set of tires for this car." The governor thought a moment and finally offered his solution. "We don't need new tires, Will," he said. "What we need is a new chauffeur."

Although he readily fined himself twenty-five dollars for being late for court and fifty dollars for killing a turkey hen instead of a gobbler, he nevertheless waited some years after electricity was available before getting his house wired, and then would have only one base plug installed.

Once asked what he considered the greatest thing he did for the people while governor, Governor Miller replied, "It was a thing never publicized and seldom mentioned; but it was the proclamation I issued in March, 1933, declaring a bank holiday in Alabama." Characteristic of his thinking, he added, "It saved the state from bankruptcy. And it was done eight days before Roosevelt declared the national banking holiday."

Sooner or later the group under the pecan tree would recount stories about Lummie Jenkins.

Up until 1927 Camden couldn't keep a town marshal, because every Saturday night, toughs from across the county would come in and beat him up. When Mayor E.W. Berry pinned the badge of marshal on Percy Columbus Jenkins, Lummie made a vow that he'd take on all troublemakers, but with bare knuckles, not guns. "We had a lot of fights till I won respect," Lummie recalls, "but they were fair fights and I won them all."

After serving for seven years as marshal, three as deputy, Lummie was elected sheriff of the county and he held that office for thirty years. In all that time he never wore a sidearm. Suspects readily turned themselves in when sent for, because they knew they would get fair treatment and protection in his care.

Before his law-enforcement career, Lummie learned a valuable lesson about what kind of fight not to get mixed up in. One cold winter afternoon he was changing trains at the small station of Nadawah, eighteen miles from Camden, when a fistfight occurred between two men, both strangers to Lummie. One was big and heavyset, the other a little shrimp of a man. When Lummie saw that the big fellow was making mincemeat out of the little guy, he walked in, pushed the little fellow back and took on the big one all on his own. Lummie admits that he had already had a bracer or two with his buddies before leaving the train and felt like he could whip a pack of wildcats.

Shortly a crowd gathered around, but instead of intervening, they just sicced the two on. Lummie was having a rough time, face battered, lump on his head, and clothes ripped and bloodied. But he wasn't about to give up. Just as he was getting his second wind, a shot was fired, by whom no one would disclose; but Lummie knew for a fact where it landed. In his arm, shattering the bone.

This ended the fight, but not Lummie's ordeal. By this time his train had come and gone, so he set out walking those eighteen freezing miles to Camden in the black night, nursing his broken arm. "On my way," Lummie says, "I fell in the creek and my clothes froze stiff. But that experience taught me a lesson, never to get mixed up in a ruckus that wasn't any of my business, especially with a man bigger than me."

Lummie had the reputation of never losing his man. One such incident concerned a man named Willie Brown. Willie, drunk and angry with his girl friend Essie Hall, slashed her so badly that her entire body was mutilated, one kidney being completely excised. Sure that Essie was dying, Willie fled from his home in Pinehill, finally making his way to New Orleans. Even though Essie, nicknamed "Hash" because of her carving up, recovered, Lummie never forgot the incident. One day eighteen years later while he was in a filling station in Pinehill, a girl came in and laid her mail down on the counter to eat an ice-cream cone. On one letter the return address read: "Willie Rogers, 219 N. Roman St., New Orleans, La." Lummie had a hunch that Willie Rogers was Willie Brown—a hunch that set wheels in motion that led to Willie Brown's identification, arrest, and final conviction.

One of Lummie's prime pleasures was locating shinny (moonshine) stills and catching the operators. Having discovered a still one afternoon with no one present, Lummie hid in the bushes waiting for someone to show up. About nightfall two men arrived, one already feeling like he owned the world. While Lummie waited to see if anyone joined the two, the talkative one, leaning against a tree, pretended to crank up a telephone and begin a conversation. "Hello, Central," he began, "gimme Mister Lummie." After a pause, "This you, Mister Lummie? Well, I sho wish you wus here. We're having a fine ole time, Mister Lummie. Better come and have a snort with us."

In the midst of loud laughter from the two, Lummie emerged from the bushes and said, "All right, Buddy. Here I am."

"Lord God, Mister Lummie," the man gasped, "you sho got here in a hurry."

On occasions a federal agent would come in to help clean up the county stills, which kept the county fairly well lubricated in spite of its voting dry year after year.

One time Lummie and an assisting agent went to the Peach Tree area near an isolated Negro community, where Lummie suspected a still was hid. Sure enough, a tell-tale wisp of smoke led them to it. Cautiously they approached. On such occasions Lummie took a shotgun along, not as a weapon, whose blast in the air might halt a fleeing suspect. There were two men, whom, for a wonder, Lummie did not know, minding the moonshine. Lummie decided that being two against two, a quick rush-in, along with a call to halt and a shot in the air would be their best tactic.

The agent and Lummie dashed in, but when Lummie called "Halt!" and shot, the moonshiners, instead of halting, lit out in different directions like scalded hounds. The agent, soon hopelessly out-run, lost his man. Lummie overtook his, lunged, and grabbed him by the leg and threw him down. But his grip was not firm enough. The suspect broke away and was gone again. But in the scuffle, the man dropped his hat. Lummie picked it up, and widening his hunting range, he came upon a cabin, a woman and children out on the porch, all big-eyed from fright at hearing a nearby shot. Lummie had a sudden inspiration.

"Whose still is that down in the hollow?" he asked the woman.

"We don't know nothing 'bout a still," she said.

"Well, I just killed a man down there. Here's his hat," Lummie said, tossing the hat onto the porch.

The woman screamed and caught her head in her hands. "Lord," she screeched, "if that ain't Alphonzo's hat, for shore!"

By that time the neighbors, who had heard the commotion, were gathering. Yes, they all knew Alphonzo. He lived right behind the woman's house. So everybody went out to look for the body. In the course of the search, Alphonzo was found alive and well, hiding in a crib. With the help of his prisoner, Lummie was soon able to locate the other suspect. When it was all over, the federal agent could only shake his head and remark: "Well, I'll be damned!"

One other time while Lummie was watching a still, the owner came in and readied a fire for lighting. The wind was blowing, and his matches kept going out without igniting the sticks and leaves he had piled under the boiler. As this process continued, Lummie crept closer, until he stood directly over the crouching figure. Finally as another match was struck, Lummie leaned over and said, "How 'bout a light, Buddy?"

Startled, the man looked up and, recognizing Lummie, fell back in a dead faint. When he came to, he sat up and shook his head. "Jesus have mercy," he said. "Mister Lummie, I thought you wus a ghost."

The men who regularly loaf under the pecan tree in fair weather often move into the barber shop in foul. Camden abounds with people who enjoy kidding each other as well as strangers, and Clarence Ward was such a one.

One cold rainy day a stranger came into that male sanctuary and asked where he might buy a pint of liquor. Feigning sincere concern, Clarence told him to go down the street to Matthew's hardware store on the corner and ask for Mister Bert Sessions. "Mister Sessions," Clarence assured the stranger, "will be glad to let you have all you want."

The stranger went out pleased, not knowing that Bert Sessions was not only a pillar of the Methodist church but a prohibitionist of the first order. The stranger had no trouble locating Mister Bert, but when he stated that he'd like to buy a little bootleg liquor, Bert exploded, gave the stranger a piece of his mind and invited him to get the hell out.

The stranger, realizing that he'd been "had," hurried back to the barbershop. "Where's that S.O.B. who told me where to get some liquor?" he shouted. "I'm gonna beat hell outa him."

The waiting men were hoping for just this. "That fellow just walked down the street," they told him, "but if you want to stay alive, you better leave him alone. He's an ex-prizefighter, and he'll mop up the sidewalk with you if you so much as spit in his direction."

The stranger thought this over a moment and stormed out, got in his car, and screeched out of Camden.

Sharp traders, both those who win and those who lose, elicit either praise or sympathy from the loafers' bench. On one occasion, however, it was a case of even-Steven.

Bob Charley and Lum Bago, names changed to protect the guilty, were friends and farmers, both of whom had a weakness for trading, and both priding themselves on driving a sharp bargain.

One day Bob was over at Lum's place, and among several horses and mules, saw a mule that struck his fancy. "Lum," he said "I'd like to have that big red mule over there. How much you take for 'im?"

"Hundred and fifty dollars," said Lum.

"Give you a hundred," said Bob.

"Hundred and twenty-five."

"Hundred, cash on the barrel."

"Sold," said Lum. "Send me a check and I'll deliver the mule."

Soon after the check and mule were exchanged, Bob Charley, hot as a hornet, lit out to find Lum.

"You blankety-blank old coyote," said Bob, "why didn't you tell me that mule was blind?"

"You didn't ask me," said Lum.

Knowing a trader's code of honor, "buyers, keepers," Bob licked his wounds and bided his time.

Some months afterward when Lum was riding over Bob's pasture, he spied a bull he liked and needed.

"What you take for that bull?" Lum asked.

"Not for sale," said Bob.

"Well, if you ever want to sell him, I'll give you a hundred dollars for 'im."

Some weeks later Bob sent Lum a note. "I've decided to sell that bull. Hundred dollars, cash."

Lum came over shortly, gave his friend the hundred dollars, and went down in the pasture to get his bull. Posthaste he returned, red in the face and sputtering with rage. "You dirty so-and-so," he foamed, "that bull's dead!"

"I know it," said Bob.

"Damn it, why didn't you tell me?"

"You didn't ask me," Bob answered.

Buck Tait was known as a shrewd horse trader. On the other hand, his friend, Harry Ray, considered himself an expert judge of mule flesh. Needing a mule, Harry hoped to buy one from Buck but expected to have to do it the hard way. After looking over Buck's mules, he settled on a strong black which he liked, and examined him with satisfaction from teeth to tail.

"How much?" Harry asked, patting the tethered mule on the shoulder.

"Hundred dollars," said Buck readily.

Astounded at the moderate price, Harry hastily agreed to take the mule and shook hands on the deal. Nevertheless, Harry became uneasy about Buck's willingness to sell without dickering for an hour or two. "Now that we've traded," Harry asked, "just why did you part with that mule so easy?"

"Well, there's two good reasons," Buck answered. "One is he's the devil to ketch; 'nother is, when you ketch 'im, he ain't worth a damn."

All henpecked males get a sympathetic ear under the pecan tree. There was an old farmer who doted on his foxhounds and fox hunts, but as the years passed, he became so hard of hearing that he could not enjoy the sweet music of his hounds, Old Tick and Old Tack. His wife squalled at him continually and begged him to get a hearing aid. Finally he did so, but because he refused to wear it except when he went fox hunting, his wife was infuriated, scolding him day and night about refusing to wear the appliance in her presence. At last he told her, "If you ever shut up, I'll put the damn thing on and listen to you."

On another occasion the same ole fellow admitted to his cronies under the pecan tree that the reason he came in and sat with them so often was that "It hurt me so bad to watch my wife split the kindling and bring in the stove wood."

Bubber Moore might easily win the title of Camden's cleverest wit. He could usually top the best raconteur with some spontaneous remark that was often the perfect squelch.

Bubber himself liked to tell of an experience he had in World War II. It was a Saturday afternoon, when his buddies were heading to town for whatever diversions they could find, that Bubber was stuck with the detail of stoking the barrack's furnace for the afternoon.

The more he thought about what he was missing, the more he hated the idea of sitting in the basement shoveling coal into that furnace every half hour. At last he hit upon an idea. He'd just put the whole afternoon's supply of fuel on at one time and go on to town.

When he returned that night, he soon learned that in his absence the boiler had blown up and the barracks was as cold as an igloo. Bubber admitted that from then on all he did to help win the war was peel potatoes.

During the time when work was proceeding on preparations for a new post-office building in Camden, passers-by congregated about the ever-deepening and widening excavation for its basement.

One day an on-looker asked the question: "Why in tarnation are these folks digging such a deep hole?"

Answer came from another: "Shucks, didn't you know? That's where they're gonna bury all the S.O.B.'s in Camden."

Bubber, who was standing by, dryly commented, "Will you tell me, please, who's gonna cover 'em up?"

Some people gather stories like wool britches pick up beggar-lice. Leslie Johnson, otherwise known as "Les," was such a one. If he stopped by to tell a tale himself, someone was likely to recall others about him. Though banking was his business, he was probably better known for his expert fishing and hunting.

In time, his reputation spread to a considerable circle of city friends, bankers and businessmen, who besiege him with requests to take them hunting. Consequently, what with getting up before day in the mornings and entertaining his guests by night, by the time turkey season ends, Les is a walking zombie.

On one of these hunting trips, Les and an amateur hunter friend had been waiting under cover in the woods for hours on a cold spring morning with Les attempting to yelp up a gobbler. (Les had previously warned his companion of the necessity of being perfectly still.) At last, with both men half-frozen and half-paralyzed, Les saw a big gobbler step warily into sight and within shooting range.

Out of the corner of his mouth, without moving a muscle, Les whispered to his guest, "There's your turkey down the path."

The visiting hunter whirled around, asking excitedly, "Where? Where?"

"Yonder he goes," sighed Les, pointing to the old bird sailing majestically into the woods.

On another occasion Les took an elderly woman into his office to discuss a loan, one with which she intended to add a bathroom onto her house. Since the woman had never before borrowed money from his bank, Les asked her the customary question, "Aunt Mary, before now, where have you been doing your business?"

The old lady put her hands over her face and ducked her head. "Why, Mister Les," she said, "you oughta be 'shamed o' your self for asking me any such a question."

Just around the corner from the pecan tree and a stone's throw from Dr. Paul Jones' clinic was, until recent years,

Brownlee's (the Negro undertaker's) funeral home. As someone commented, Brownlee was Doctor Paul's only competitor, Doctor Paul trying to save 'em and Brownlee hoping he wouldn't. Besides a hearse, Brownlee operated an ambulance, and some folks accused him in fun of riding around with a doubtfully injured or ill case in hopes his passenger wouldn't make it to the doctor until too late.

On one occasion, at least, bringing in a badly injured and unconscious victim, Brownlee decided to wait around and see which way the dice would fall. The patient received a blood transfusion and was stitched up, revived, and got off the operating table under his own steam. When Brownlee saw him, his face fell. "Doctor," he said, "you did me wrong. That was my man, now look at him."

There was a saying among the more superstitious blacks that when someone encountered Brownlee on the street with his little black dog in tow, you better watch out, death might be close at hand. Once Dr. Paul's secretary, partly in fun, said to one of the doctor's notorious dead-beat patients, "If you don't dig up some money for the doctor, I'm going to sic Brownlee on you." Walking alone down in the business part of town, the man noticed that Brownlee and his little black dog were behind him. He quickly ducked into the hardware store, and in sauntered Brownlee and his dog. The man hurried out and vanished into the drugstore, and in came Brownlee and his little black dog. That did it. The man fled down the street to his landlord, borrowed fifty dollars, and made haste to Doctor Paul's office. Paying his long-standing debt, he earnestly begged the secretary to "For God's sake, call that gravedigger and his dog off my trail."

Once late at night, Brownlee went out in the backwoods to pick up a body. As was customary, he had a helper who rode with him. While Brownlee was in the victim's house attending to burial details, a neighbor of the family asked the helper if he could ride back to town with them. "If you don't mind riding in back with a stiff," was the answer. The man's need must have been urgent, for he accepted the offer and climbed in back, unknown to Brownlee.

Just before reaching Camden, when Brownlee slowed down for a right-angle turn, the passenger in back started banging on the partition and calling, "Stop! Stop! Here's where I git out!" Instead of hitting the brakes, Brownlee rammed down the accelerator, the car dashed across the road, tearing down guardrails and jumping the ditch. Fortunately, they all came out alive—all, that is, except the corpse.

The men under the pecan tree never tire of talking about hunting, fishing, dogs, and whatever game is in season. Here is where they bring their turkey beards for comparison, bring in their fox tails, their deer, their biggest catches of fish, the longest rattlesnake, the biggest bobcat, often taking pictures for future proof.

When it was discovered that sending an electric current, generated by an old crank-type telephone, into the water would cause the scaleless fish, stunned by the shock, to surface and they could then be easily caught and hauled into boats, fishermen went wild catching catfish by, as they called it, "telephoning for them."

When strangers dropped by the pecan tree, the men had no end of fun betting them that they could catch a boatload of fish merely by telephoning them to come up out of the water. Many bets were made and lost, always to the consternation of the newly initiated. But as the news spread, the method of thus catching catfish was so abused that, in time, it was outlawed.

But the practice did not subside, the pecan-tree sitters say, until the deacons of the Presbyterian church had caught all the catfish in the river for church suppers, and all their generators had been dumped overboard to destroy evidence.

Nothing tickles the pecan-tree sitters more than an incident in which Uncle Sam goofed or got a dunce cap clapped on his head.

Hence they often recall with relish how the almighty federal government, instead of extracting the last drop of blood from one of its poor tax-paying slaves, for once practically buried

him in free, easy money in the matter of a few days.

Customarily, William Lawler received a yearly government check, for a modest amount, as payment for not planting certain cotton acreage. But one happy morning, near the last of the week, he found his post-office box stuffed with government checks. This was great. He was having considerable fun telling his friends about his windfall, when one of the postal clerks called to tell him he had a bushel basket of mail and would he come and get it since his box wouldn't hold it all.

By this time the folks downtown had heard about William's good fortune and came by to congratulate him, while William himself, busy counting his money, had been unable to work. The post office was closed over Sunday. When it opened on Monday morning, a clerk called William to bring his pickup truck—literally, no fooling—to get his mail, for he had mailbags full, more than all the clerks together could handle.

William looked at his mountain of mail, realizing that it would take a week or two just to open the envelopes, and somehow the fun began to turn serious. What was he to do with so much money? Tomorrow it might be a boxcarful. While people were congratulating him on becoming a millionaire, William began calling for help. One of the banks allowed him to haul his mail bags full of checks to its confines for safe keeping until the Washington office could be notified. Supposedly, its first move was to feed some sort of stop order into its computer, which had been so generous. The agents who came to retrieve the checks would not believe the need for a truck to haul off the largess until they saw the mountain of mail with their own eyes.

As it came, so it went. For a few days William had possessed a fortune, just how much he would never know. But it would have pleased Camden people more if it had been "for real" and not just a blooper.

A correspondence between a Washington bureaucrat and a

now deceased overseer on the Gee's Bend project in Wilcox County, a bold experiment in rehabilitating this all-Negro community during the Great Depression years, still gets laughs under the pecan tree whenever it is mentioned. Though doubtless fabricated in part, it symbolizes the often asinine directives coming down from Washington to the man in the field.

After the Gee's Bend project had been in operation for several years, some enterprising statistician in Washington, thinking he had uncovered a glaring omission in the supervisor's report, wrote him as follows:

"Dear Sir: It has come to my attention that after five years of operation your project fails to show any increase from the mules owned by your farm families. Please look into the matter and send in corrections for our files."

The supervisor, assuming that the only increase one could refer to as derived from a mule was one of production, answered: "Dear Sir: I request you examine records which show a reasonable increase in farm commodities where mules are owned and employed."

The eager beaver in Washington was quick in challenging what he considered a plain evasion of his question. So he wrote again: "Dear Sir: My recent inquiry concerning increase from tenants' mules was not in reference to production but reproduction. If in five years you have no offspring to show from these animals, I suggest you secure the services of a good jackass."

To which the supervisor replied, hastily and hotly: "Dear Sir: I hasten to inform you of what I assumed any fool ought to know; namely, that a mule is a critter without pride of ancestry or hope of posterity. But if you think a jackass could remedy the situation, just come right on down."

If a group of fox hunters is loitering under the pecan tree, the talk is probably about fox hunting. Among them, no other sport is worth mentioning.

Occasionally local fox hunting is pursued on horseback, but it is usually done in a much more relaxed manner. The hunters, who are an intrepid breed indeed, gather up their hounds (which they dote on as if they were child prodigies), meet at a place likely inhabited by fox, and release their hounds to hunt on their own.

The hunters build up a fire and sit around it, on stumps or logs, and listen to the music of the chase. Each hunter knows his dog's tongue and from various inflections he can deduce the heat of the race, whether the dogs have struck a fox, a deer, or in shame, a rabbit; which dog is leading the pack and which has gone astray. At this safe distance great claims can be made, without being challenged, for each dog's nose, cunning, and stamina.

When the baying indicates that the fox has been holed up or treed—a gray fox will climb a tree when hard-pressed—the hunters follow up to find the quarry. That is, if they are so inclined or able. Actually, they hope the fox will escape so that he may be hunted again and again, and many old foxes do just that, evading their pursuers by doubling back over their old tracks, crossing streams and highways, or wallowing in carrion or manure.

But the most important feature of the hunt is that mellow meeting of men of like mind for a few idle hours out in the open, ideally under a moonlit sky, away from carping women-folk and with every man's favorite bottle handy. A non-fox hunter can only imagine the joy of these outings. One of the racy ingredients common to all is the tall tale.

Of all tales they may tell, few could surpass the one told by hunter Judge Leon McCord about the fox that set the world afire.

A character, the judge relates, known as Tight McGuire, a native of the North Alabama hill country, was so addicted to fox hunting that the bay of a hound would set him off at any hour of the day or night.

One winter night McGuire heard the baying of his hounds. He sat up in bed to listen, pulling the comforter about his shoulders. But the music was irresistible. Out he leaped and into his clothes. He saddled Old Paint, swallowed a snort of brandy—to ward off pneumonia—and took off in the direction of the music.

It was one of those clear, cold mountain nights. The frost was thick. The moon looked like a pot of gold. The cry of the dogs grew fainter as the fox led them far from the road. The hunter waited for the hounds to circle back. Again and again they crossed the road. He moved on, watching them go first to the right, then to the left.

Ever and anon Tight required just one more sip of liquor. The moon slipped below the hill. A wind rose. It was getting colder. Suddenly the music went into a questioning key. The fox had outwitted the dogs. They had lost the trail.

Sadly, Tight decided to give up the race and go home. Just then the sun burst above the horizon. The whole frosty earth turned a glorious red. The hunter stopped, thrilled by the sight. Oddly, there was a rustle in the bushes by the roadside. Tight looked down and into the road tip-toed a tremendous red fox. He was panting from hours of exertion, but on his face was the foxy smile of victory over his traditional enemy.

Hunter and fox together gazed into the fiery glare of the sunrise. Tight took another swig of brandy and looked at the fox. The fox looked up and eyed the man contemptuously.

"I wish you'd look a-there," the animal finally said, lifting his paw toward the east. "I've run so far and I've run so fast that, dadburn my red-haired soul, I've set the whole world on fire!"*

On and on these stories go, old and recent, offering a glimpse of these usually happy-hearted people.

*Permission given by Bill Ladd to reprint this story as recorded in the *Louisville-Courier Journal*.

TWENTY-TWO

Separate and Unequal

After World War II, I went back into the classroom, this time in a school that was modern and adequate. But what I thought would be a diversion from housekeeping came nearer to being the death of me.

My official duties consisted of teaching three classes of English, one double section in seventh-grade social studies, one eighth-grade history, and supervising one physical education class and one study hall. My fringe benefits were putting on plays and chapel programs, attending all athletic events, band concerts, and dance revues, designing posters, decorating floats, and helping with and chaperoning social events.

My history class needed two of me; one to scrub the cobwebs off my mind, one to teach. My English classes needed four of me: one to teach grammar and spelling, one to teach composition, another to teach literature, and one to grade papers. I still had the old-fashioned notion that in order to put words together sensibly, one must keep on putting them together; also, I preferred question-and-answer tests rather than the true-false kind. But once all this blizzard of paper work erupted, I, unfortunately, had to correct and grade it.

The physical education class needed somebody else, not me. I hated to play games, particularly the kind that required dashing about and hitting something or other and in turn getting hit by whatever was hit. I knew about as much about the rules of these bat-ball things as a turtle knows about flying. But one does what one has to do, or gets a smart pupil to do it for him.

Imagine being shut up in a room with fifty thirteen-year-olds to whom you were supposed to dispense some knowledge. Just keeping order would have required a whole police force. But the information which I was supposed to teach in this social studies class was not of earth-shaking importance, so we wandered far afield, exploring natural phenomena from the lowly ant to the stars. We enjoyed the diversions more than the text.

In tests, many of the children gave me back as good as I gave them, some even better. These made some of the trouble worth while. The definition of a farmer as given in the text was: "A farmer is a person who makes his living either directly or indirectly from the soil." Asked to define a farmer, one little fellow, who came from a small cotton farm (cotton farming was fearfully rough about that time) gave this answer: "A farmer is a person who can't make a living either directly or indirectly from the soil." I scored him 100.

We had been studying breeds of cattle: Hereford and Angus for beef, Holsteins for quantity of milk, the Jersey for butterfat, etc. To the question: "What kind of cow produces the most milk?" the answer was, "A heifer."

In my history class I was surprised to find a number of children with big lumps of bitterness inside them about the Yankees and the Civil War. A few still defiantly defended the Ku Klux Klan. I assumed there were klansmen among their kinfolks.

To a question concerning the cause and result of the Civil War, I received an answer something like this: "The cause of the Civil War was because the Yankees didn't like slaves and we did. So they came down here and made us turn them aloose. But the Ku Klux Klan rose up and made them behave themselves."

To a question about the Revolutionary War came an answer that would have been greatly welcome had it been true. "We didn't like to pay taxes to the British," this student said, "so we decided to fight. George Washington had a hard time, but he finally won the war. The result was we didn't have to pay taxes anymore."

World War II was not yet recorded in the textbooks, but we undertook to review it briefly. I learned from one little fellow that the person who started the war was "Heil Hitler" who wore a "swat sticker" on his arm.

The English courses were in higher grades, and never was

heard such moaning and groaning over outside reading, homework, or written assignments.

Grammar? "Who needs it? Nobody writes any more. Who cares about a split infinitive or a dangling participle? What the devil is an infinitive, anyway, or a participle? We don't wanta be Shakespeares, for Pete's sake." But some learned a lot about putting down words so as to make sense and using commas where they should, whether they wanted to or not; and these thanked me later for their being able to pass freshman English in college.

Poetry? Ho, hum and ho, hum again. "That silly stuff? Always talking about love or dying." And would they memorize just a few stanzas here and there? "Horrors! Knock your brains out today and forget it tomorrow? Let the girls do it, if they want to. Not us boys. Stand up and recite 'How do I love thee?' or 'Build thee more stately mansions, O, my soul?' Oh, my soul, is right."

Interestingly enough, we had a good time in literature. There were things that competed favorably with *Mad Magazine* and Mickey Spillane. And strangest of all, we had the best time with *Hamlet, Macbeth,* and *The Merchant of Venice.* The girls loved *Romeo and Juliet,* but the boys? "My aching back! Killing yourself for love? That's for the birds."

And study hall. Fifty or sixty students. All very different people. The two boys with heads together checking a diagram? They were figuring how to rig up a generator that would be driven by the windmill they had built. One day both would be electrical engineers. The boy sketching on scratch paper? No, he wasn't studying, but one day he would be an artist. The one with the owlish glasses reading *War and Peace* would be a medical doctor. The one teasing the girl next to him would be a banker. The one with his head down on the desk? No, he wasn't asleep. Just bored to death. One day he would be a professor of engineering struggling to teach students as bored as he had been. The boys with hay on their jackets and mud on their shoes were already young farmers and would learn more in the field than in their textbooks to make them the bigger and better farmers they would become. Others would choose other careers, and the girls would later be nurses, teachers, secretaries, along with being mothers.

Thinking of these, I recall another boy from my earlier teaching. A quiet, blond-headed boy. I once returned one of his papers with this comment: "I can't grade this paper because I can't read it." He is now an actuary and vice-president of a big insurance company.

Two years of teaching made my housekeeping duties look less arduous, so I turned the classroom over to younger hands, more able to cope. The most I did for these boys and girls was to love them. And I still do.

This school in which I taught, though not a great school, was, within certain limitations, a good one. And it was loved. It was an all-white school and was supported with concern and considerable pride. But there was another school in Camden, over on the hill. It was the Negro school, all black. The two did not meet. They were as separate as if they were on different sides of the world, and they probably differed as greatly. Right or wrong, that was the way it had always been.

Although teaching trades to slaves was early undertaken on southern plantations, slave owners generally frowned on teaching the three Rs. In 1832, in fact, the Alabama legislature enacted a law making it a crime to teach a Negro to read or write. An attempt at public schooling for blacks did not come until some time after the Civil War. Even after public education was established, funds were not available to support a dual school system properly; and since whites were dispensers of tax monies, they consistently allocated a larger per capita share of school funds to the white schools. Thus it was in Wilcox, if not in other Black Belt counties.

As early as 1896 the Supreme Court ruled in favor of the separate-but-equal schools, and an amendment to the Alabama constitution in 1901 provided for such schools, but for many years little was done actually to remedy the disparities between black and white schools in Wilcox County. Black schools, back then, often ran no more than three or five months, teachers were paid twenty-five dollars a month, and attendance was irregular, if at all. Gradual improvement had, of course, taken place in later years, but only after the *Brown vs. the Board of Education of Topeka* case in 1954, which voided the old separate-but-equal doctrine, was a concerted effort made to bring the black schools up to the white level. More and better schools were constructed for the Negroes, black teachers were paid on a par with whites, and various instructional aids were provided. But it was already late, very late, for black children to catch up.

Then in 1964 came the Civil Rights Act which decreed integration of schools, and in 1967 Judge Frank Johnson ordered all schools, not already complying, to do so. Meanwhile, school authorities in Wilcox County, acting on the wishes of the majority of white school patrons, feinted and dodged, beating back the inevitable with court case after court case. True, there was a compromise effort made toward gradual integration that might have succeeded had it been acceptable, but the court turned it down.

In 1971 a district judge, presiding over one of the many hearings concerning our schools, remarked with considerable pique, "Hell, I've integrated all the schools in South Alabama, and Camden is still here dragging its feet."

In 1972, after a prolonged boycott by blacks, integration finally came. No piece-meal, gradual process, but the whole system all at once. As a result, parents of white children did what they have done in many communities across the land, they built and staffed a private school. Most parents who could afford it enrolled their children in this school, and teachers left the old school as readily as the children. Other private schools went up over the county, carrying more white children with them.

The vacuum thus created in the public schools was filled with Negroes, causing some schools to become almost black again. Because of this abrupt change, at first a sort of schism was created between whites who could afford the private schools and those who could not. Parents of the latter resented the cleavage which seemed to maroon their children on an island outside the white community. Some children went elsewhere to school, a few white families moved away, but in spite of the sacrifices they must make, most whites now send their children to the private schools, which are good schools indeed.

To avoid integration was not the only provocation that prompted whites to provide separate schools for their children. There was a related reason; whites feared that the level of achievement required in their schools would be lowered, in what would become predominantly black schools, in order to accommodate the majority. Though the long-time, unfavorable socioeconomic status of the Negro was reason enough to account for the gap that statistics indicated existed between the standards of black and white schools, the fact that the lag existed posed not only a problem but a reasonable fear.

Perhaps Wilcox County became somewhat derelict in its duty toward public education for blacks in the past because of a unique and most enlightened educational venture launched in the county in their behalf when public education was still in its infancy. In 1895 a group of five mission schools for Negroes was established in Wilcox County at the request of Judge William Henderson and those Presbyterian Yankees who settled here after the Civil War. These schools were identified as manual training schools since, besides a general education, they taught skills by which students might become self-supporting. All had churches or chapels, and three had dormitories for boarding students, a number of whom came from north of the Mason Dixon line. Besides these Presbyterian schools there were a number of elementary schools for Negroes supported by the Lutheran Church. For many years these schools were far superior to the state-supported schools. No wonder that a large majority of blacks attended them.

These schools are worthy of mention. Two of them were established in east Wilcox near Rose Bud and Oak Hill and were supported by the Rosenwald Fund, Rosenwald being vice-president of Sears, Roebuck and, at the time, serving on the board of trustees of Tuskegee Institute. Another was Snow Hill Institute, established through the influence of Booker T. Washington and Dr. Norton, successive presidents of Tuskegee Institute, who were aided by a donation of land by Mr. Simpson, a white benefactor. Later the Rockefeller Fund added twelve hundred acres to this donation, the revenue from which furnished financial aid to the school through the years.

People here, both black and white, will not soon forget the able, high-minded men who conducted these schools: Peoples and Wilson of the Camden Academy, Cotton of Canton Bend, Williams of Miller's Ferry, Edwards of Snow Hill, and Wilson of Rose Bud. Two of these men are buried on the campuses of the schools for which they gave lifetimes of dedicated service.

Another noteworthy school for Negroes, the Street Manual Training School, a few miles from Camden in Dallas County, was established "on faith" by Emmanuel Brown in 1904. Brown was born of an exslave and grew up in abject poverty. He says, "A Negro was considered educated in my youth if he could pass the mail-box test, that is, if he could write legibly enough for a letter to receive an answer." After passing his mail-box test, Brown wrote to a well-known philanthropist in Boston and received aid to enter Harvard, the first Negro to enter that institution.

He might have made more money up North, but like Booker T. Washington, he chose to cast his bucket down where he was. He wanted to found the kind of school he had lacked as a child. This he did, though his faith was severely tried by the difficulty of raising funds to carry on and to rebuild after three destructive fires.

These schools stood like shining candles in those murky days of early education, and their influence for good has gone far beyond the confines of the county and is still felt in the lives they touched. Gradually, however, they were absorbed into the public school system, the last being the Camden Academy, the school over on the hill.

Presently, in the public schools of the county, only a handful of whites remain. Four private schools now supervise education for the majority of white children. The high school in which I taught is now all black with the exception of a few white teachers; integration, so vigorously fought for, has not yet been achieved. Voluntary integration will doubtless come gradually and in time, for private schools are very costly, and some people are beginning to realize that a good public school system, serving all citizens alike, is essential to a community's stability and growth.

TWENTY-THREE

The Vantage Point

One of the joys of growing old is in looking back and reflecting on the goodness of God and the kindness of man. Blessings which have flowed out of friendships with young and old of our own race are innumerable and without measure, but other blessings have been ours only because we have lived in this place. These have come from our association with a host of long-time, black friends.

Besides many black men who were the back, brawn, and oftentimes the brains, of Will's activities, there are three Negro families which have so aided me in my everlasting battle against dirt, danger, hunger, and disarray, that without them, I would long ago have given up the ghost and gone to keep company with the old Confederate soldier in the cemetery.

One is the Thompson family. When I set up housekeeping in the old Liddell home, our soiled clothes were taken in a large split basket, almost filling the body of a one-horse wagon, to the Thompson home on Monday mornings. There, Lethe Thompson, the mother, boiled our clothes in the big iron wash pot, rubbed them on the scrub board until buttons popped off by the dozens, ironed them with a flatiron heated over hot coals, then returned them, spic and span, to the basket. Smelling sometimes of wood smoke, but always sweetened by sunshine and fresh air, they were ready to be fetched back home on Saturday.

The Thompson girls, Clara and Inez, cleaned house, nursed the babies, and helped cook until Mattie Davis came to take over the kitchen. The Thompson boys weeded, watered, raked and pruned yard and garden. But more importantly these boys, who were some years older than mine, acted as companions and guardians to my boys while they were too young to know danger and yet old enough to dare the devil.

Summers, after school, and on Saturdays these boys took mine camping, hunting, fishing, exploring, helping them to live a thousand boyhood adventures in safety and bringing them into the age of accountability with such a love of nature, its wild creatures, its moods, its beauty, its witchery, that they find it imperative to return periodically to woods and fields and stream to renew their spiritual springs. Pity the poor boy who has only manmade gadgets to entertain him and knows no black companion to call his friend.

Nearly forty years ago, shortly after we discarded the old wood-burning cook stove, which had to be stoked with extreme care or the biscuits and cake would come out either soggy or charred, and its attached water heater which grumbled and thundered and threatened to explode whenever the water got too hot, Mattie Davis, better known as Bea, came to our house. She took charge of the kitchen and has ruled that domain ever since. However, as nurses and housemaids disappeared, she has taken over their duties as well. As anyone who knows her can affirm, Bea is a wonder.

Besides rearing, all alone, a family of five, spending half her days helping me, she is the good Samaritan in her neighborhood—tending the sick or elderly, doing their cooking, cleaning, washing, errands. She often gets tired and is sometimes ill, but unless bedridden, which is rare, no persuasion can keep her from "her job," which consists of a thousand chores at my house from doing the dishes to setting the scuppernong wine.

But I must add that in her enthusiasm for doing everything that should be done, Bea often works me to a frazzle. By her promptings she sees to it that I keep up with my outside duties and obligations and at the same time run a tight ship at home. From May to November she comes early, gathers the fruit and vegetables, sets them down before me, and announces, "Now we'll can beans and tomatoes this morning," or "We'll do pickles today." Or, "We can't let these peas and this corn go to waste. We'll have to freeze today." Then when my pantry and freezer are bulging, and I'm weary of well-doing, she'll remind me, "We got to preserve those figs or can those pears for our city chillun [meaning mine] that haven't got a butter-bean to their names." And so we do. She'll whirl in and make rolls by the dozen dozens and send me out with them to friends " 'Cause they brought us some cookies or cat fish. Remember?"

Instead of grumbling when the family gathers and makes mayhem all over the place and eats like a swarm of locusts, she beams and does her best spoon bread and stuffed turkey and sends them home with a load of goodies from our pantry, kitchen and garden.

Then the Pettway boys, Scat and Boo, whose barely known names are Felix and John. They come by, often unasked, to cut the fire wood, plow the garden, mend fences, move furniture, and do the heavy chores which we cannot do ourselves. They drive us out of town to doctors and hospitals, bring us watermelons, goobers, and fresh meat when they kill a deer or shoat, and almost embarrass us with their many kindnesses. Without their aid the old homeplace would be falling apart and our happy and familiar way of life would be doomed.

Maybe the rural Black Belt is one of the few places where such ease, goodwill, and, yes, affection, still exist between blacks and whites. But because of changing life-styles and attitudes, the ties between young blacks and young whites seem less satisfying and more tenuous. In time, however, the new generations, meeting in the same market place, measured by the same merit, may form differing but possibly even more rewarding bonds.

Another interesting thing about growing old is being constantly surprised by change; another is being surprised by a constancy that defies change. Some of the evolution in the Black Belt I have touched upon; but it is particularly gratifying to one of my sex to see one thing that has changed so little: the status of women.

Black women in the South, since slavery days, have been matriarchs in their families, ruling their domestic domains with iron wills and strong backs; white women of the Black Belt also rule theirs, particularly their menfolk, but with a velvet touch and a silken cord. They are able to do so because the men have long been conditioned to consider their women something very special: weaker, of course (they think), but moving in some loftier estate, inviolable, almost sacred, as if they were ladies of King Arthur's Court, themselves their defending knights. Interestingly enough, since men treat the women as fair ladies, the women in turn attempt to produce such an image, even while practicing their inscrutable will to dominate.

Hence, if one should ask how goes Women's Lib in the Black Belt today, I would say that the question is about as pertinent as asking a butterfly why it has wings. It doesn't know because it has always had them. Black Belt women aren't out marching and making speeches for something they have always had, in greater measure perhaps than any others of their sex in this broad land of ours. From the cradle to the grave, they are not only liberated but venerated.

Women here were put on a pedestal long, long ago, when the pedestal was made of hand-hewn logs and the woman who stood on it wore a calico apron and sunbonnet. Later she was put on a white-gold throne, where she wore rustling silk and white kid gloves. And now the pedestal is made of plastic and plywood, but it *is* there and it *is* strong, and the woman who stands there, dressed in a starched uniform or pantsuit, is almost as secure as her great grandmama was. She is there because her menfolk keep her there and everybody seems to like it that way.

From her first breath, a girl child is taught to be a coquette. She learns before she toddles how to smile and cuddle so as to be petted and told what a darling she is. As she becomes a teen-ager she learns early that her masculine admirers like her pretty, feminine, and sweet. So she practices to please. And if her escort doesn't help with chairs pulled out and pushed back for her, with wraps on and off, doesn't open and close doors for her, and willingly cool his heels for an hour waiting for her to primp, or take care that she is no wallflower at a party or dance, then he may find that he isn't welcome to take her out again.

A certain friend once found how this pattern of behavior on his part had affected his child. Her escort, having taken this friend's teen-age daughter out on a date, decided that he was fed up with waiting on girls as if they were helpless infants and that he would practice some Men's Lib for a change. Thus, after bringing his date home, he refused to come around and open the car door to help her out. She then refused to budge. The tug-of-war must have gone on for some hours, for it was two o'clock in the morning when papa went out to investigate what was going on in that parked car. To his surprise he found two youngsters sound asleep. After waking the pair and receiving an explanation for such conduct, he found himself faced with a dilemma. He could hardly blame his child for following a precedent she had learned from himself, yet he felt such sympathy for the lad that he refrained from lecturing him on his lack of good manners. He could only pretend anger for their going to sleep, while smiling inwardly at this impasse between custom and common sense.

But as the years march on, the girl child becomes a young lady, and few there be who do not entrap mates with their feminine wiles. Then it is, that the unsuspecting male, without realizing what is happening to him, becomes the total victim of the little wife. She weaves a net about him, strand by strand, each strand as fragile as spider web, but all together stronger than steel. First a baby or two. What Atlas of a man can withstand the tender entrapment of a rosy-cheeked extension of himself? Then, when the toddlers are off to school (if not before) mama goes to work and brings home a pretty hefty pay check to help pay for the house or car so that papa can buy that boat and fishing tackle he has so yearned for.

And does the little wife feed her man frozen TV dinners? Not unless she's down with pneumonia or unless he stayed out with the fellows too late the night before. She feeds him hot biscuits, chicken pie, and pound cake, fattening him up and keeping him purring like a kitten, even though she may be making a widow of herself years sooner than if she had fed him bran and skimmed milk. And whether she wears curlers during the day or goes to the beauty salon, it's because she intends to let her hair down for her man when he comes home for the night.

But as time goes on and romance cools, the man of the house may go out looking for fresher flowers to pluck, and when the little lady finds out about his wanderings, she may greet him with the rolling pin as a reminder to behave. But what does this hairy-chested he-man do? Next morning, black-eyed or lumpy-headed, he'll swear to his cronies that he had one too many the night before and fell down the stairs. Blame his wife? Never. No matter how justified he might be to do so. Now he might repeat some racy gossip about another man's wife—not in her husband's presence, however, unless he is prepared for a fight to the finish—but he'd be tortured on the rack or burned at the stake before he'd tell a smutty story about his own wife.

But, alas, the time may come when the little lady herself gets weary of well-doing and may want a fling, and so decides to part company with old whiskers for keeps. Then he will willingly swear to any sin or infidelity necessary to keep the record of his children's mother chaste. Finally he allows himself to be taken to the cleaners for the rest of his natural-born days so that the kids and their mama can live in style.

Later on, no matter how once pretty, no matter what lotions are used or vitamins taken, cheeks become wrinkled as prunes, hair becomes scraggly and gray, and backs as stiff as walking sticks. Then what happens to these little old ladies? Why, the men help them up and down, rise when they enter the room, remove their hats in their presence, pat them on the back, sometimes kiss them on the cheek, and tell them outrageous lies about how pretty they look.

The deference shown old women—pardon me, elderly ladies—hereabouts is a wonder to behold in this uncivil world. Such as this: a group of elderly widows is picked up each weekday by Miss Julia Jones and brought to town to get mail, medicine, and groceries. Now this particular car, with its occupants, is well-known to everyone in Camden. If not, it will be, for Miss Julia knows that her charges can't walk far and that she must park near their destinations. Consequently, she parks any way she can, often in the middle of the street. When cars stack up behind her, somebody usually gets the word back as to the problem, but does a hubbub ensue? Not a horn is blown, not a dirty look is exchanged, only smiles. Nobody goes into a tizzy. All just wait and wait until it's possible to squeeze into the left lane and pass.

Everyone but the oldsters themselves knows who the octogenarians are (both male and female) who drive all over the road and never look where they are going—and you may be sure they are given a wide berth. But give them tickets for reckless driving? Or revoke their driver's licenses? Of course not. They would be insulted. So they drive on and on until death parts them from this mortal danger or until some child hides the car keys and keeps them safely at home.

"Male chauvinism" in the Black Belt? Forget the dictionary. An expression never used around here need not be defined. Black Belt males docilely accept the wiles and wills of their women, somehow compensating occasionally by slipping off with their fellow sufferers for a fox hunt or a poker session, or to get soused, to make them feel as tall as trees and as strong as Paul Bunyan. Black Belt men believe that women were made for loving; and though they may not all be Clark Gables, they'll go to hell and back for their womenfolk. And the women love it and want to keep it that way.

Another surprise a person gets as the years heap up is in seeing how many times he has been wrong in the past. So it is with me.

Yes, Camden is a gossipy place. But not in the sense I had thought. What passes for gossip is most often just "people news." People are the most important things here, and naturally what happens to them and what they do gets talked about. As much complimentary and happy as derogatory. If one backslides or falls from grace, he is quickly and heartily forgiven and accepted back into this family of folks. After all, by middle age everybody and every family have experienced so many slips and slides that they rarely condemn them in others. There are often rumors that are untrue and malicious, but bearers of this sort of gossip are usually known for their excesses and their stories are given little credence.

Was Camden eager to tar and feather the unorthodox or the nonconformist, as I had feared? If he is a strange outsider, a zealous do-gooder trying to save us from our sins or to mold us into an alien image, he will be in trouble; but cranky homefolks are either patiently humored or quietly tolerated. I hadn't lived here long before I learned that no matter what the carper said, thought, or did, Camden would go right along doing as it darn well pleased, letting the devil take those who heard a different drummer.

And how did my uneven self fit into what I supposed was a rigid, square-angled mold? Evidently none cared whether I fit or not, and most seemed to accept me in spite of myself. Only once, after being unlucky enough to have a little book published, was I told that I should leave the county and never come back. True, my astonishment at such advice did make me want to leave, but being unable to do so, I could only wish with Job that mine adversary had written the book instead of me. (At the time, I swore that I'd never repeat such a venture, but here I am trying again. But should anyone wish me removed elsewhere, may I suggest a little patience. After all, I'll soon be leaving anyway, and when I go, I'll be gone for quite a while.)

The kindness and compassion of these people, I have already recorded. But for sure Camden was not as straight-laced and smug as I had thought it was. Such an appearance was only a thin veneer. For looks only. Like movie makeup. Peel off the roofs of all these homes, large and small, and you will find under them all the courage, the sadness, the loneliness, the loveliness, the griefs, the fears, the pettiness, the foolishness, the bitterness of all mankind.

The suffering of a thousand souls is no greater than the deepest suffering borne by a solitary person; love of a thousand hearts is no greater than the love of the one who loves the most. It is all here, not in mass, but in fragile, vulnerable, one-by-one "ordinary" people: the young couple whose baby girl was born without limbs, who have made her the angel of their lives instead of the destroyer; families who have lost beautiful young sons and daughters in highway crashes, who have picked up their broken lives and forged ahead on faith; a family losing a young son under the blades of a brush cutter; a child succumbing to leukemia, or a young mother to cancer. No blame, no cursing fate, no bitterness of soul. Acceptance, resignation, hope! A helpless spastic tenderly cared for, lifted, carried, rolled; a ninety-year-old widow in precarious health, rejecting all attempts to put her into a nursing home, carrying on her business by telephone; the diabetic who lost limbs, now driving a car and working again; an elderly couple, each determined to live in order to care for the other, finally dying within days of each other.

Under one roof you would see the lovers' joys and fulfillment, under another the anguish of separation or the heroic struggle against drug addiction or painful disease; tears for a loved one's departure into the long night; the love and loyalty of family and friends; the coping, the caring, the sharing. They are all here.

Through the years I have come to love this little close-to-nature place, every stick and stone of it. I have put down roots here. It is home. It's music is sometimes disturbing and in a minor key, but most often it is gentle and melodious. Its people are members of my larger family, and I love them, every one: the wise, the foolish; the good, the not-so-good; the odd, the ornery. I am some of all of them, and they are all parts and pieces of each other. Somehow we understand the strange harmony made by a people who, like diverse instruments in an orchestra, are in tune with some master chord.

Something is here that "brook does not know nor flower hear nor cloud understand." But a listening and hearing heart will surely find that something if he lives here long enough.

TWENTY-FOUR

The Weaver's Shuttle

The years marched on, too swiftly for comfort. The old house grew more comfortable. Will and I grew more comfortable. Not having fires to build, ashes to take out, wood and kindling to bring in for feeding eight cavernous fireplaces, having a thermostat to do our furnace-stoking for us, with gadgets all over the place to do for us what we had once had to do for ourselves, was living in a different world from the one we were born into.

The children grew up, finding their pleasure in hunting, fishing, and riding horseback by day and doing their courting in cars and at the movies by night, instead of staying home and playing the piano and making love in the old porch swing. In spite of the floor walking by their elders, they survived and finally went off to school, allowing some peace and quiet to settle over the old house at last.

It was foreordained that they go to Auburn University, for Will and all of his brothers had attended that institution back in those benighted days when the entire student body assembled in Langdon Hall for chapel, when all boys took R.O.T.C., and when coeds were scarcer than ducks in a desert. The children probably absorbed their father's enthusiasm for Auburn by osmosis, but their interest was won by the stories he told about professors and personalities connected with the old "cow college."

During Will's years there, Doctor Drake was the college physician. Aside from occasional real illnesses, the boys were often forced into undiagnosed maladies by problems and pressures inflicted upon their minds rather than their bodies. Doctor Drake could usually detect such ailments and prescribe accordingly. The boys said that he carried a coat pocket full of variously colored pills, and after thumping their chests and making them say "Ah—ah," he would reach into his pocket, lift out a handful of red, white, green, and yellow pills, hold them out in his palm, blow the dust off them and then pick out one with this remark, "Take this, young fellow," he'd say. "It should have you back in class tomorrow." Most often the boy was back, all right, and doubtless the pill went down the drain.

Dr. B. B. Ross was head of the chemistry department. The boys called him B_2 $Ross_2$. For an experiment one day to record chemical reactions when two chemicals were mixed, he prepared two flasks of clear liquid, one of them hydrochloric acid, Will recalls. Dr. Ross held up the two flasks and announced solemnly, "Now, boys, watch carefully. When I pour these two perfectly clear liquids together, the resulting solution will be pitch black."

As he poured, the mixture turned blood red. What Dr. Ross suspected had indeed happened. One of the boys, who had previously flunked the course and knew what was prepared for this experiment, had substituted one chemical for another having a different reaction.

Professor Ross set the flasks down. In a dry nasal twang he remarked matter-of-factly, "You may record in your notebooks that experiment number ten was a failure. Reason being, some jackass has been fooling with the stuff."

The following incident occurred in Dr. Petrie's Latin class when Will's oldest brother Roy was in attendance.

Since the Latin class was scheduled immediately after the noon meal, there were always some sleepyheads dozing during recitation. On one occasion when the students were giving the principal parts of verbs, Professor Petrie, on noticing one head on the back row nodding, called on its owner to recite. The student whose name was called woke with a start and nudged his nearest neighbor, whispering, "Whadda he say? Whadda he say?"

His inattentive companion answered out of the corner of his mouth, "Damn-if-I-know."

In perfect form the dazed student rattled off, "Damifino, damifinare, damifinavi, damifinatus."

"Damn-if-he-didn't," commented the astounded Dr. Petrie, and went on with the lesson.

Once a freshman, undergoing hazing, was made to shave his head, leaving a fringe of hair around the edge to look as much like Dr. Petrie's bald head as possible. Also, he was made to sit on the front row directly under the doctor's eye.

At roll call, Doctor Petrie, recognizing himself, decided to hand the joke back to the class. "Well," he said, "I see a new Dr. Petrie here today, so I'll just step down and let him take charge of the class."

The flustered boy hesitated, but quickly recovered. He rose and came forward, making this announcement: "Class dismissed!"

Dr. Petrie acknowledged his delegated authority and let the dismissal stand.

During the days when the specter of socialism was scaring conservative people into fits, a funny thing happened periodically in our family, whenever Will's uncle on his mother's side would come to visit us. Uncle Ernie Ricky, with his ramrod posture and his Kaiser Wilhelm moustache, was as soft-spoken and kind as he was hardheaded and opinionated. One of his unforgivable sins was that he was an avowed socialist. But he turned sin into crime by going all over Camden preaching the virtues of socialism to anyone who would listen. The whispered fuming within the family over this indiscretion was a joy to behold. The redeeming thing about Uncle Ernie's theory, however, was that three times in his life he had entered into a communal, worker-owner sort of enterprise, though every time the venture failed. When asked what happened, he would say, "The idea was right, but too many members turned out to be rascals."

Besides being a socialist. Uncle Ernie was that unmentionable, unthinkable oddity, an atheist. He once told me why. In early life, when his devout parents prayed without avail to be released from debt, he decided there was no God and kicked over the traces, living and working wherever fortune beckoned.

Once when he was working in Mobile, where my mother was living at the time, she invited him to dinner. As there was no other man present, Mother asked him to say grace. "You'll have to excuse me, Mrs. Goode," he said, "but I do not believe in the supernatural." Mother all but collapsed at such a shocking statement. So stunned was she that she forgot the blessing she had said for seventy years and got down to "Give us this day our daily bread," before realizing that she was saying the Lord's Prayer instead.

In deference to the family's feelings about such matters, Uncle Ernie kept quiet on religious matters. But he didn't keep quiet about evolution. He carried pamphlets and pictures to substantiate his belief that man came, if not from the ape, at least from some other subhuman species; and he had quite a fine time talking about such a possibility to anyone who would listen. But when he attempted to plant this idea into some of the young minds in the family, he got black marks from their elders, even though he may never have known it.

One perverse satisfaction I got from Uncle Ernie's visits was proof that all the maverick kin were not on *my* side of the family.

The World War II years skimmed our little town of its able-bodied men, who were scattered over the face of the earth. We kept our ears glued to radio boxes, we bought bonds, we sent cookies, we wrote letters, and we prayed. Our boys, many of them, just done with flying kites and shooting squirrels, were flying over Germany, bombing it to smithereens, air-chasing Rommel over the African deserts, clawing their way up the Italian boot, wading onto Normandy beaches, fighting their way through France to Berlin, island-hopping across the Pacific, five at one time pinned down on the shores of Iwo Jima. When telegrams arrived telling us of this one or that missing, or gone forever, the whole town closed up and everyone went home to grieve. Most came back with scars that healed, but some had deeper wounds that would never heal. Some still carried buck-eye balls or rabbit feet in their pockets. Others arrived with Flying Crosses or Bronze Stars. Still others returned under the flag they died for.

Here at home we suffered only small privations. We never went hungry. If our food-ration stamps gave out, there were always large Negro families who could spare us some. Women guarded their silk hose as if they were spun gold and lack of gasoline sent us out at times on shoe leather, or kept us at home. But no one complained. Camden was, and still is, patriotic to its marrow. Should anyone hereabouts spit on Old Glory or burn it, I daresay he would not remain in Camden to do it again.

One thing that occurred during the war is still happily recalled by my family. Since pleasure riding by car was out of the question, Will found an old topless buggy, brought in Old Mamie, the retired ice mule, hitched her up to the buggy, and we were in business for getting about town. On cold winter afternoons, with me driving, the children and dogs piled in under laprobes, the children and myself capped and scarved, we clip-clopped through town in our dilapidated rig, much happier than if riding in a limousine. Judge McLeod, our probate judge at the time, unable to recognize us as we drove through town all muffled up, assumed we were poor benighted souls who must surely be penniless, half frozen, and on the verge of starvation.

The judge mentioned the heart-tugging scene to his friends at our church, where he was an elder. "I think we ought to take up a purse," he suggested, "for this old lady with a pile of children who drives through town in a broken-down buggy behind an old mule. They must be cold and hungry and need help."

Suddenly the light dawned on Will, who happened to be one of the men present. "Let me pass the hat, Judge," he said. "because that's my family."

Another not-so-happy event occurred because of the wartime shortage of gasoline. When forced to ride the bus to Selma one day, I found the back of the bus crowded with Negroes while I was able to choose my seat from one of several vacant ones up front. Standing in the aisle beside me, holding onto the luggage rack, was a young Negro woman, very much pregnant. Being alone on a double seat, I leaned over and told her I'd be glad to have her sit down beside me.

She thanked me graciously and sat down. The bus driver slowed down, turned and said to the woman, "You'll have to move. That seat is reserved for whites." "But it's all right with me," I protested. "Maybe it is with you, lady, but I drive this bus and the rule is, she ain't to sit there," was the driver's ultimatum.

This was a small incident, but it angered me. Laws were for making people behave. This was not only one of special privilege, but it denied a human kindness. Later I recounted the incident among friends. "After all," one remarked, "it was the law, and you were wrong in breaking it." Then I shocked myself when I said, "If so, the law needs changing." "And when it is changed," came the answer, "you'll be the straphanger." Eventually this prediction did come true for many, but it was also not uncommon for Negroes of goodwill to offer their seats to white women or the elderly.

One of our local reference points in time will, for many years, be the flood of 1961. Nothing like it had happened since 1896, and few residents remained who could remember back that far.

The weatherman explained the late February rains by saying that a cold front had collided with a warm front from the Gulf and each refused to give way to the other. As a result, one deluge after another descended on Alabama and North Georgia. The creeks rose with such shocking haste that whole herds of cattle were swept away; others, escaping, were marooned on knolls or hilltops.

As the Coosa and Tallapoosa rivers rose, flood warnings went out for the Alabama River, but at first they were not alarming to us in central Alabama. While government helicopters were busy airlifting hay to stranded animals, and barges bringing out those in danger, local farmers felt themselves lucky to have time to get their livestock onto safe ground—safe, that is, so far as anyone could remember.

But the weather remained warm and springlike, the skies periodically clearing like a May morning only to blacken and descend again in drizzle or torrents. The river kept rising, dangerously at last, creeping, deceptively demure, over the face of creation. Roads went under, then whole pastures, then bushes and fencerows. Finally, trees disappeared in the calm, shimmering sea. And the predictions were for more rain yet.

People would and did move their livestock before moving themselves, refusing to believe that the water would go where it had never, in memory, gone before. But when houses in the lowlands began to be the centers of ponds, the men in Camden—bankers, preachers, lawyers, farmers—all set out to do what had to be done. As in the evacuation of Dunkirk, every available boat and skiff was commandeered and "Rescue Backwater" went into high gear. People first, then other things in order of importance.

The evacuation of scores of Negro families was an epic to warm the hearts of the most cynical: white men bringing out Negro children and old folks in their arms, helping mothers and babies into and out of boats, then returning for a load of trussed-up hogs and goats, chickens (if they could be caught), and even squally cats tied up in gunnysacks. Last but not least were the mongrel dogs. The last boat to cross the water, now fifteen feet deep over our swampland, was Bob Lane's pleasure boat, loaded with hounds, all sitting bolt upright, their ears cocked and tails wagging, happy as larks to be part of this strange new adventure. "What a pity," someone remarked, "that Huntley and Brinkley couldn't have their cameras here now."

After the people were safe and sheltered, men turned their attention to stranded livestock, which were now endangered. The highest bit of land on our riverfront was a sandy field, once the site of an Indian village. On a few acres here were huddled a hundred and fifty cows, calves, mules, and horses belonging to both whites and blacks. The skies had finally cleared, and the air was much cooler. The weather had changed at last. If the river rose only inches more, as predicted, the livestock would escape the water, and feed could be boated in to them.

It was a beautiful springlike morning, March 5. I remember it well. Before going to church we had walked about the yard admiring whole flocks of camellia blossoms, which had burst into bloom during the warm, rainy days. Feeling tremendously relieved after days of anxiety, we went to church to give thanks for our special blessings. Midway the sermon, a farmer neighbor came in, tapped Will on the shoulder, and beckoned him outside. What happened then must have given the preacher a shock, for first one and then another of the men in the congregation got up and followed those two. Shortly the preacher was left with nobody but women and children to preach to.

What had happened we learned soon enough. A radio message had come through that the dams above us, to keep from bursting, were being forced to release their pent-up waters.

These waters would raise our already monstrous river two feet more. This rise would cover the sand-field. If the livestock could not be rescued, they would drown or soon die of pneumonia.

Frantic calls went out for help. But government barges were too busy up above evacuating people to be concerned with livestock. So the men who left church that Sunday, together with their Negro friends, went to work building a fence around the animals so that when the water covered the area the animals could be caught and would not stray off into swift current and be carried away. Posts had to be carried over, holes dug, wire stretched and nailed, but by nightfall two miles of fencing surrounded the helpless animals.

One concerned Negro working alongside Will said to him in some distress, "Mister Will, you're fencing these critters in. How they gonna git water to drink?" His question relieved the strain. "By morning, Sam," Will assured him, "these critters will have the whole Alabama River to drink."

It was an agonizing night. We slept hardly at all. Every available man was ready to go by daylight, and if not busy swimming out other livestock, was concentrating on this group on our inundated knoll. A government barge finally arrived, but its shape posed a serious problem. It was half-moon shaped, ends sitting high up out of the water, built to back up to banks and take on cargo. Here there were no banks, only a gradual slope under the water. Consequently, the animals could not be driven into the barge; they had to be hoisted aboard. But what man or group of men could perform such a feat?

It was at this point that someone went to Camp Camden and gained the release of the ablest prisoners, all Negroes, and brought them across the water to help. Fitted with lifejackets, they were the happiest helpers outside of iron bars. There was no color line or class line here that day. No load was too heavy, no cow too obstreperous to handle.

The younger animals were lassoed, caught, trussed, and bodily heaved over the side of the barge, where they were

tethered to ropes and rings inside to keep them from stamped-
ing to either side and capsizing the vessel. Horses and mules
were no trouble. They were tied to outside rings along the
barge's sides, where they could be kept swimming, heads
above water, across the two miles of water to dry land. The old
cows, frightened and excited, went berserk. That is, until it
was found, if driven into deep water where struggling was
impossible, they could be lassoed from motor boats, haltered,
then, like the horses and mules, tethered to the barge and
swum out.

Leslie Johnson and Bill Jones were two who had an un-
forgettable experience that day. Bill was driving one of the
motor boats; Leslie had lassoed a frantic old cow and was trying
to get a halter on her when suddenly the motor choked down.
The cow's tail had become entangled in the propeller. Just
then the old cow found solid ground underfoot and lit out to
rejoin her companions, dragging boat and men behind her like
the tail of a kite. Unfortunately, between her and her intended
destination was a sizable thicket of youpon and haw bushes
with branches as spiny as cactus and stiff as wire brushes.

As Les and Bill were being helplessly ripped and shredded
in this thorn thicket, Bill yelled, "Cut 'er tail off, Les! Cut 'er
tail off!" As Les remarked later, "Did you ever try cutting a
cow's tail off with a pocket knife?" But, superhuman effort
often does meet dire emergency, and the tail did eventually
come off, and though raw and bloodied, Les and Bill could
begin again to rescue the now bob-tailed old maverick.

By nightfall all the animals (some of which were their
owners' only possessions of value) were safely enclosed on
high ground; while the men went home exhausted and cold,
some to develop pneumonia, but all happy over a job well
done. The prisoners, given a bonus and a shoat to barbecue,
were the only ones who were sorry that the rescue was over.

Though losses from the 1961 flood may have been less in
Wilcox County than in urban areas upriver, they were
nevertheless very real and heart-rending. As the waters rose,
small animals, particularly rabbits, were driven in droves to the

islands. Boys, black and white, skipped school to go hunting them with guns, sticks, and bottles, bringing in the little creatures by the boatload. Pitiful though their fate, their meat, which might have been lost, was not wasted. For days on end evacuees ate rabbit stew and fried and barbecued rabbit. No one could know how many quail, squirrel, turkey and other kinds of wildlife were destroyed. But when the water did recede, after twenty-eight days at floodstage, roads and fences were clogged with debris and dead animals, some brought from miles upstream. Dead limbs and tree trunks were caught in upper branches of mud-coated trees still standing, and left hanging there. Occasional carcasses of cows, horses, and sheep caught in the forks of trees dangled grotesquely twenty, thirty feet from the ground. In places where whole herds perished, bulldozers pushed them into piles or gullies and burned or buried them. Burial vaults from country cemeteries bobbed out of the ground, many floating away, their cargoes never to be properly identified.

Cover crops were lost for a year, pasture grasses were rotted and overlaid with a slimy film of mud, with winter weather far from done. Virginus Jones, like other hard-hit farmers, had no patience with any Pollyanna-like consolation about his loss. When he bemoaned the devastation on his place to a friend, the friend suggested that he should be thankful for the rich sediment deposited over his land. "Man," answered Virginus, "if I were able, I'd make you eat every damn grain of the beautiful stuff."

Though local, these catastrophes seemed to usher in the most tragic, divisive, yet awe-inspiring decade in the memory of living man. Small and isolated as it was, Camden felt the shudders of national tragedy and the pride, suspense, and joy of national achievements.

TWENTY-FIVE

Swift as a Shadow

After the Selma-to-Montgomery civil-rights march, the civil-rights drama moved from the Deep South to a wider stage—North, East, and West—augmented by resentment of the war in Vietnam, and marched across the land with a heavy tread. Black frustration, long-smoldering, flared, and was fought with fear and bitterness.

On November 22, 1963, President John F. Kennedy was assassinated. This tragedy seemed to unleash furies—marches, riots, bombings, murders, all mixed together and heated by ugly sights, inflamed words, and wild rumors. The witches' brew boiled and bubbled, then exploded. On April 4, 1968 Martin Luther King was felled, as Kennedy had been, by an assassin's bullet. Dr. King's death marked the climax of the greatest social struggle since the Civil War and resulted, indirectly at least, in putting vast reforms on the statute books of the land. But, as in an earthquake, the aftershocks continue—even today, long after the curtain of Act Three came down. Will Act Four bring more tragedy? Or will our people, working together, find a better way to reach real brotherhood?

Soon after Dr. King's death, Senator Robert Kennedy was slain, and still later Governor George Wallace was struck down. The latter's partial death was followed by Watergate. Appearing at first as a shadow, Watergate proved to be the tip of an iceberg of colossal proportions. Our ship of state, heading toward it in a fog, shuddered and listed on impact but, with a wrenching effort, righted itself and continued on course.

Shock, disillusionment, despair accompanied these tragedies, until it seemed that words of goodness or gladness were no longer heard in the land. Instead we felt with Yeats:

Things fall apart; the center cannot hold;
Mere anarchy is loosed upon the world,
The blood-dimmed tide is loosed, and everywhere

the ceremony of innocence is drowned;
The best lack all conviction, while the worst are full
of passionate intensity.

But like a pox that erupts at the height of fever, in the midseventies the rash began to subside. Has a healing process begun? In our bicentennial year we took time to assess the damage and weigh the good. We felt more vigorous than before. We sensed that greatness had been with us all along, even while we moved in delirium.

Little Sputnik, circling the globe in 1957, led the adventure in space. Satellites and space vehicles, tossed into the skies, circle the moon and visit the planets. Armstrong made that giant step for mankind onto the moon in July 1969. Wonders of technology made our lives ampler and easier. Rather than want, our danger became overindulgence. Instead of working ourselves to death, we had to conquer idleness.

Ecology went to war on pollution and waste. The Pill was introduced to fight the population explosion. Young Americans picked up the dusty Christian banner and marched across the land with a new look and a new voice. Eighteen-year-olds went to the polls and voted along with blacks, and did not, as some had predicted, turn the world wrong side up.

The fruits of medical research, applied by doctors, were keeping more and more of us alive past our Biblical three-score-and-ten and past the time when some of us would be better off gone. Those who have been so blessed or cursed, as the case might be, have seen farm labor advance from pay of fifty cents a day to more than two dollars an hour, and skilled labor earn more in a day than most of us once earned in a month. We have leapt from the horse and buggy to the jet; we have seen the garden and chicken house picked and packaged and put in the deep freeze; seen skirts sweeping the floor shrink to a ruffle around the waist and stretch again to below the knee. We have seen bustles and stays sitting in prim parlors change to halters and hiphuggers walking the streets; bathing beauties formerly attired in blouses and bloomers peel down to a fig leaf and a smile; Victorian prudery buried under an avalanche of frankness and freedom; while the cook and cradlerocker now go out from their homes to rock the world. Through all the upheavals, it had been a great time to be alive.

The dream of visionaries back in the 1930s for a navigable waterway from Mobile to Rome, Georgia, is at last becoming a reality. In 1963 the lock and dam, together with a powerful power plant, was begun at Miller's Ferry, the front door to Camden. Engineers and workmen, jokingly called the "dam people," moved into Camden. Some liked us well enough; others, though disapproving of our racial attitudes, would nevertheless refuse to allow a Negro nurse to mind their children.

Finally the lock and dam were finished. The twenty-two-thousand-acre basin behind the dam quickly filled, forming a beautiful lake, named Lake Dannelly in memory of our late Judge Bill Dannelly. Lakeside houses sprang up over night and fishing and watersports began to rival the sport of hunting. A place of towering pines on the lake shore was chosen for a public park; now next door we have a spot like those we used to go hundreds of miles out of state to find.

Even before the dam was finished, a great paper mill, MacMillan-Bloedel, coming from faraway Canada, lighted down beside the river in the middle of our pine forests and began cutting and planting trees for more miles around than most of us had ever traveled. Prices of land and timber went up, and "land po' " people now became land- and timber-rich. More people arrived, and natives were hardpressed to keep tab on them. No longer did everyone know everyone else or speak to everyone, or suspect them merely because they were strangers.

A silk mill sprang up and white women and black women sat down to sew side by side, no longer taking notice of skin color. Black clerks appeared in stores, black deputies were hired to help keep the peace; and black patients now looked out from immaculately white sheets in our hospital and nursing home—a tenant next door to his landlord, a maid next to her mistress, receiving similar care and kindness.

Through the years Camden has undergone transplants and facelifts that have made it look younger by the year. The business section is now neat and trim, old homes have been renovated, fences have been taken down, lawns have been landscaped and planted with every tree, shrub, and flower that thrives here, particularly the queens of the South, the azalea and the camellia. Subdivisions, peopled by whites, sprang up like toadstools after a rain; new Negro developments mushroomed about the town's rim, with all-electric homes spilling over with black faces before the paint on the houses had dried. Cabins on plantations, deserted, fell down almost before their chimneys cooled.

Cattle growers from colder climates have brought their herds here, where they can graze them the year round. Soybean farmers have come from the midwest, to where they can harvest two field crops a year instead of one. Banks, businessmen, and folks needing jobs are delighted, but many Camden people look with "pickle faces" at all these new people and this new growth. They want us to stay as we are. Hunters and nature-lovers want Camden to stay forever a country town surrounded by fields and untouched forests. Dyed-in-Dixie Rebels are afraid that the newcomers will change us so that we won't know ourselves any more and will try to tell us what to think and where to go.

But whether one wishes it or not, after a Rip Van Winkle sleep of a hundred years, a new day is dawning in our sky. Swift as a shadow, it is moving across this drowsy little land.

On a shelf in our kitchen the family has placed small, dead and discarded things discovered about the yard and garden: a black beetle with menacing claws, cicada shells split down the back, snail shells and seashells, a wren's nest, a snake's rattle, a shark's tooth, a hawk's claw. One fall day while removing dry stalks from a flower bed, I found a small gray cocoon with something inside that rattled dully like the kernel of a dry seed pod. The cocoon was added to the collection on the shelf and soon forgotten.

Months went by. One balmy day, when the world outside was gay with blossoms and fresh green, my eyes caught a movement, a flutter, among our little dead things. I looked, unbelieving. There was a wondrously lovely creature, weakly waving two huge satin wings, pale green, tinged with gold, above a glistening body barely supported on wobbly legs. Immediately I examined the cocoon. There was a hole now, and the dry, dead thing inside was now alive and free, a moth of indescribable beauty.

Maybe this is what is really happening to our little, long-cocooned corner of creation, which I like to think of as a Place of Springs.